products of his society, age and culture, or whether an author and his works can create a new culture and lead to social changes. None of the prevalent theories can be ruled out, as there are plenty of evidences in favour of either of the aforesaid theories. Books are, therefore, having immortal values, both as mirrors of contemporary society and culture, as well as powerful tools for social reforms or revolutionary changes. A few classic examples of such books may be referred to in this context, viz., H.B. Stowe's *Uncle Tom's Cabin*, M. Gorky's *Mother*, Pearl S. Buck's *Good Earth* or Karl Marx's *Das Kapital*. We may also refer to some such books from Bengali literature—like Dinabandhu Mitra's *Nildarpan* or Bankim Chandra Chattopadhyay's *Anandamath* or Sarat Chandra [illegible] these books had long-felt impact [illegible]. Books are thus [illegible]

[illegible]

Books, Libraries and Culture

About the Book

It is a book on books and their traditional abode like libraries, both of which contribute to develop the culture of a nation. To have a wider perspective of the main focal theme and to establish co-relationship between the books, libraries and culture, an overview of culture with its various manifestations, along with the story of evolution of books and libraries are presented to the readers. As public library movement is a continuously developing process, the author has tried to visualize Library Vision 2020 in India.

To appreciate the multi-faceted characteristics of modern public library concept, various aspects of the subject are elaborated in different articles. Particular emphasis is given on Community Information Service (CIS) which is gaining world-wide growing importance and is now considered to be immensely needed in Indian scenario too.

To further develop the focal theme, critical areas of modern book preservation and oft-quoted apprehension of digital divide and so-called threats to printed books and reading habits are also analysed in detail. In fine, the collection of articles aim to attract readers' deeper interest and attention towards books and libraries that will eventually enrich our cultural heritage.

While concluding, a glowing tribute is paid to the first Indian National Librarian through which the author wishes to formulate an innovative Five Principles of Librarianship.

About the Author

Dr. Barun Mukherji, born in Calcutta in 1933, comes of a distinguished educationist family of West Bengal. Dr. Mukherji, B.Sc, M.A., Ph.D., B.Lib.Sc., a specialist Librarian in profession, was also associated with teaching in Library & Information Science in the Rabindra Bharati University, Kolkata. He was long associated with public library movement and is presently the President of Bengal Library Association, as well as the President of the all India professional body IASLIC (Indian Association of Special Libraries and Information Centres).

Since his college days, he was attracted to socialist ideology and patriotism of Netaji Subhas Chandra Bose. He was a Member of Parliament (Rajya Sabha) from 2006 to 2014. He was also a member of Parliament Library Committee. He is well known as a Netaji researcher and has some reputed publications to his credit. He also made exhaustive study on the History of Early Printed Books.

Books, Libraries and Culture

Dr. Barun Mukherji

CONCEPT PUBLISHING COMPANY PVT. LTD.
NEW DELHI-110059

ISBN-13 : 978-93-5125-114-9

First Published 2015

Published and Printed by

Concept Since 1974

Concept Publishing Company Pvt. Ltd.
A/15-16, Commercial Block, Mohan Garden
New Delhi-110059 (India)
T: 25351460, 25351794, *F*: 091-11-25357109
E: publishing@conceptpub.com, W: www.conceptpub.com
Editorial Office: H-13, Bali Nagar, New Delhi-110 015, India.

Cataloging in Publication Data—*Courtesy:* D.K. Agencies (P) Ltd. <docinfo@dkagencies.com>

Mukherji, Barun, 1933- **author.**
Books, libraries and culture / Dr. Barun Mukherji.
pages cm
Includes bibliographical references and index.
ISBN 9789351251149

1. Books and reading—India. 2. Libraries—India. 3. Public libraries—India.
4. India—Civilization. I. Title.

DDC 028.90954 23

Dedicated
to the memory of
the First Indian National Librarian
Late B. S. Kesavan
who first inspired me to undertake
Study on Books

Preface

As a post-graduate student of Literature, as well as of Library & Information Science, and being associated with public library movement since long, I have developed a keen interest on 'Books' which leads me to study various manifestations of Culture. In fact, this study further encouraged me to correlate books, libraries and culture. With this humble background, I have had various occasions to write articles or to deliver lectures on multi-faceted aspects of Books, Libraries and Culture. When the output of such writings and speeches assumed a considerable volume, I felt an urge to put them together in a book format. But the main inspiration, as well as an affectionate push to proceed in the matter came from one of my most promising post-graduate students Shri Kishore Krishna Banerjee, who has now reached a respectable position of Director General of Raja Rammohun Roy Library Foundation under the Ministry of Culture, Government of India.

The credit of the present publication thus goes mainly to Kishore who took all the trouble to make a selection of my writings and hand them over to the experienced hand of a reputable publisher like Shri Ashok Kumar Mittal of Concept Publishing Company Pvt. Ltd., New Delhi.

While releasing the book to my readers, I must, of course, admit that I could not avoid repetitions of some points, as it is a compilation of several articles, written at different times, each of which claims to be complete in itself. Hence, I seek the indulgence of my readers to accept it as an unavoidable excuse.

I acknowledge with thanks the role of various professional and academic bodies which offered me the scope to deliver Presidential address or Memorial lectures or to contribute articles for their seminars and magazines. Notable among these institutions and learned bodies are the Bengal Library Association, Indian Association of Special Libraries and Information Centres, Raja Rammohun Roy Library Foundation, Rabindra Bharati University, Vidyasagar University and others. My best compliments for their year-long enterprising activities.

My endeavour to publish the book would be rewarded if it at least can create interest among the professionals and other readers to proceed further for implementation of some of my proposed public library service schemes like Community Information Service. I believe, C.I.S. can be the most dominating prospect for future India.

TRIPARNA, Flat C/7/3,
39A, Gobinda Auddy Road,
Kolkata - 700 027

Dr. Barun Mukherji

Contents

1

Books, Libraries and Culture

A Brief Overview

Man made books, books made libraries—a combination of which develops its culture. Books are knowledge in print which in turn provides an exposure to cultural heritage of the people or the country. Manifestation of culture of a nation can be witnessed through its religions, customs, manners and food habits, costumes, music-dance and festivals, architecture and paintings and many other such ways of life. Among all these manifestations, books in print, rather the publications of the particular country are one of the strongest media through which we can visualise the culture of that country or nation.

The term Culture can be defined in many ways. A critic of 'Culture of India' defines it—"the term Culture refers to a state of intellectual development or manners. The social and political forces that influence the growth of a human being is defined as culture.

> "Indian culture is rich and diverse and as a result unique in its very own way. Our manners, way of communicating with one another, etc., are one of the important components of our culture..." ['*Culture of India*', Ram Shankar Singh, Delhi: Mukund Publication, 2008.]

India's culture, like others', as stated before, includes its religions, family customs, Indian costumes, food habits, festivals, dances, modern and classical music, theatre and cinema, Indian architecture (including those traced in mountains and caves or as found during Muslim period), Indian painting, language and literature—which includes books of various periods, and others.

To further elaborate the concept of Culture, very often authors refer to its dictionary meaning, as well as the UNESCO interpretation. The Dictionary gives its meaning as the "training and refinement of mind, taste and manners, the intellectual side of civilisation". As per UNESCO interpretation, culture is usually "interpreted as Art. We speak of culture in connection with the behaviour of people, its moral values and human relations. We denote it by action, behaviour and attitude, considered useful for the interests of society or of a certain social group".

Social anthropologists further elaborate it by distinguishing between 'material' and 'non-material' culture. The former includes technology, art forms, architecture, material goods and equipments used in daily life, in household, agriculture, trade and commerce, warfare and other social activities. In the latter ('non-material') are included the literary and intellectual traditions, beliefs, myths, legends and other forms of oral tradition. In a broad sense, then, culture is that complex whole which includes knowledge, belief, art, morals, law, custom and any other capabilities and habits (including production of books) acquired by a human being as a member of society. [Ref. *Facets of Indian Culture*, ed. Kalpana Rajaram, New Delhi: Spectrum Books, 2003.]

Books and libraries are the vehicles of culture which enrich a nation. Production of books in India has gone through a series of evolutionary stages, beginning from manuscripts to printed books, which again are now digitised challenging the threats of age-old decay. Still there are libraries which are scientifically preserving the manuscripts made with palm leaf, bark of trees ('bhurjapatra'), papyrus, starch-coated cloths ('namabalee'), parchment and hand-made papers. The culture of teaching and learning was carried out in ancient days with the aid of these manuscripts which were preserved by various indigenous methods. India still proudly bears the traditional glory of the manuscript-age which is a testimony of India's cultural heritage. The present day elite print culture emerged from the earlier manuscript-age folk culture, both of which are still available in some libraries maintaining a link between the two. This is a unique feature of some of our heritage libraries. Our manuscript-based vernacular literary culture gave rise to post-renaissance elite culture flourished by European art and techniques.

Expanding the idea further with reference to nineteenth century books produced in Bengal in vernacular language, we may have a fair idea as to how socio-cultural features of a particular time can influence the production of books at that point of time. In the arena of Bengali literature we have simultaneously seen very rich productions of classical Bengali prose and poetry like novels of Bankim Chandra Chattopadhyay, as well as poetry of Madhusudan Dutta, while on the other hand appeared the light-spirited "Battola" literature.

Libraries can very often be the store-house of culture as depicted through the books they collect. It is like a mirror through which is reflected the philosophy and life-style of the people, their sentiments, sorrows and joy, their music and poetry, their love and aspirations, their thoughts and creative productions—in fine, their culture as a whole. Thus books and libraries establish the link between the people and their culture.

The Nobel Laureate poet Rabindranath Tagore was not only a great writer, but was also an intensive reader and an ardent lover of books and libraries. In his classic discourse on 'Library', he paid tribute to the noble role played by the library in assimilating together all the great as well as the conflicting thoughts and ideas across the ages and boundaries of different countries of the world. The reader entering a library is placed at the cross roads having his freedom to go to any of the pathways of his free choice. Nobody is there to prevent the reader to make his own choice to taste the prevailing cultural expositions of varying colours and composition. Thus a library stands as a link between the books and culture. But this big process and mechanism of linkage is enacted within the shelves of books stored in a library amidst a profound golden silence comparable to that depth of silence as can be achieved by silencing the roaring waves of all oceans like a sleeping child.

While admitting this unique characteristic of books and libraries as a documented manifestation of culture, one very debatable pertinent question often arises as to the people's right to access to the libraries. Different libraries in different countries have varying experience in respect of public access. A detailed study of the people's right to access to public libraries must be of great interest for proper evaluation of books and library culture. Just for an example, we may cite the experience of Norwegian libraries in this respect. I quote: "there are two historical influences that link the many different types of libraries. One is the fellowship among the professional staff in respect of their core competence in organising, retrieving and disseminating knowledge and culture. Another is the ideological bond that all types of library and all librarians share in fulfilling the task of making knowledge and culture accessible to the public. These have been the *raison d'etre* of the librarian and the hallmark of the professional librarian. It is exactly this basic fellowship of ideology which is now being challenged by the emerging market oriented logic. The most pressing question facing the libraries today is whether the traditional social role of the public and university libraries, which emphasises free access to knowledge and information, albeit in an updated form, will retain its hold in the library scene, or whether the information administrators' agenda will gain the upper hand." [*Knowledge and Culture—Norwegian Libraries in Perspective*. IFLA, 2005.]

In the backdrop of all these discussions on the meanings and interpretations of culture, along with the evolution of book-production and public-library relationship, we may appreciate the value and role of books and libraries as an important expressive system of culture and establish interrelationship between books, libraries and culture.

2

Concept of Culture and Evolution of Books and Libraries

I

Books, Libraries and Culture—all these three are interrelated. One helps creation of the other, one leads to growth and development of the other, one influences the nature and character of the other. In such a process of mutual help and care, Books, Libraries and Culture have been continuing their life cycle from the early days of civilisation—immensely benefiting humanity and its society as a whole.

Once we endeavour to discuss about libraries, obviously books would be our prime concern and in no way allowing us to ignore the society and the people. In fact, the impact of public libraries on their neighbouring society has always been a much talked-about subject and has constantly involved us to explore the possibility of its development. Community Information Service (CIS), a vibrant theme of modern public library services, has thus occupied our careful attention to trace its evolution through decades in different countries and to discuss its present status and future prospects for the growing needs of the society and the people.

Not only an individual, but a nation as a whole is known by its culture, which is a manifestation of its way of life as well as its intellectual creativities. Beginning from an individual's life style, food habits, dresses, housing patterns, customs and festivals, even his moral values, or values of life and intellectual pursuits—all such human activities bear the distinct imprints of his culture, which is mostly integrated with the national tradition, Man lives with his tradition and derives inspiration from his inherited culture. But it is not static in nature. Culture often undergoes changes with the impact of new thoughts and ideas, but this change becomes a healthy phenomenon when it can perfectly assimilate the incoming thoughts and ideas.

II

Culture generally has two aspects. One is 'material', and the other is 'spiritual'. Buildings and cottages, architecture and art objects, dresses and clothing, indigenous agricultural techniques and tools, etc., as made by man are the material aspect of his culture and civilisation. On the other hand, its spiritual aspects are manifested in his world of thoughts and ideas, his literary creations, his tastes and behaviour, his humanitarian feelings, etc. Although culture varies from age to age, country to country or from one region-based cluster of people to other, still culture has an overall universal character and human face. It develops from the grassroots level of common people and is influenced by the folk-culture, folk-life style and their daily living pattern in a particular area or region. In spite of some inevitable outward differences between the rural and urban culture, there must be some inherent harmony between the two, otherwise that will lead to decadence of culture.

Dr. S. Abid Husain, the renowned Professor of Philosophy and Literature at Jamia Milia, New Delhi has explained the term 'culture' from different standpoints and has suggested its four meanings.

He says, most commonly the term 'culture' means—'good taste and refined manners'. He further suggests that it also means – 'material embodiments of good taste and refinement'. Accordingly, we may refer to the "buildings, gardens, and paintings of the Mughal period" as relics of the "Mughal culture".

Again, according to Prof. Abid Husain, "collective institutions, codes and systems" are also known as cultural objects. Hence, the "political and educational system of the Greeks" and the "legal code of the Romans" are often regarded as their respective cultures.

Lastly, Prof. Husain adds, the term 'culture', has also the general connotation—"a system of ultimate ends or norms of life".

Now, if we look back closely on these four meanings of the word 'culture', it will be evident that the concept of culture is very closely related to that of 'ultimate values'.

In fine, according to Prof. Abid Husain, the term culture may be explained as "the sense of ultimate values which a certain society has and according to which it wants to shape its life".

This explanation, as given above by Prof. Husain, refers to the ideal aspect of culture. The collective complexes (i.e., state, society, art, science) which are permanent results of the attempt to create ultimate values could be regarded as its objective mental aspect, the qualities and attitudes of individuals inspired by these values as its subjective aspect, and the physical objects in which these values are embodied, e.g., buildings, pictures, etc., would be its material aspect. [*The National Culture of India*, by S. Abid Husain].

Following this explanatory definition we can say that books and libraries are best examples of material aspect of culture. Going one step further we can say that books may be regarded as both subjective and material aspects of culture, as the books are embodiment of author's thoughts and ideas. Thus books, libraries and culture can be regarded as a whole a product of one integrated idea which has a permanent value in our society and civilisation.

III

In this context, we may concentrate further on the books. Books are treated as one of the richest products of culture. But at the same time, books are often found to influence the culture. There is no end of the debate as to whether an author and his works are products of his society, age and culture, or whether an author and his works can create a new culture and lead to social changes. None of the prevalent theories can be ruled out, as there are plenty of evidences in favour of either of the aforesaid theories. Books are, therefore, having immortal values, both as mirrors of contemporary society and culture, as well as powerful tools for social reforms or revolutionary changes. A few classic examples of such books may be referred to in this context, viz., H.B. Stowe's *Uncle Tom's Cabin*, M. Gorky's *Mother*, Pearl S. Buck's *Good Earth*, or Karl Marx's *Das Kapital*. We may also refer to some such books from Bengali literature—like Dinabandhu Mitra's *Nildarpan* or Bankim Chandra Chattopadhyay's *Anandamath* or Sarat Chandra Chattopadhyay's *Pather Dabi*. All these books had long-felt impact on the then society of the respective countries. Books are thus on various counts adorned through ages and are being conserved for continuing public uses. But the number of books is ever growing and for their proper conservation and public utilisation we needed public libraries. Books are thus produced and libraries are erected, both of which are intimately connected with culture.

Incidentally, we must not forget that books had never been of any static nature. They had undergone an evolution through ages, earmarking a sea-change in their concept as well as their formats or structures and obviously, this evolution of books has always been a very interesting study. The guiding force behind this evolution may be summed up as changes in technology of book production, as well as the spirit and object of book production. One of the spirits has always been the urge for democratisation of people's right to access to books, which greatly facilitate access to world of knowledge, information and pleasure. Taking clue from this spirit of evolution of books, the UNESCO Public Library Manifesto 1994 proclaims UNESCO's belief in the public library, being a store-house of books, as a living force for education, culture and information and, as an essential agent for the fostering of peace and spiritual welfare through the minds of men and women.

Before the introduction of books in its present form, we have had a long history of manuscripts which were usually hand-written by the authors themselves or by the appointed writers or 'Pundits' under the patronage of benevolent kings, landlords or priests, making use of various writing-materials like Palm leaf, Bhurja Patra, clothes or the Papyrus, Parchment, Vellum, etc., as were available in various places of the world. Meanwhile, thousands of years rolled and eventually writing materials were replaced with the advent of paper which gave a big impetus to the production of quality printed books.

Here, we may pause a little to turn our eyes to the history of early printing beginning from Gutenberg (1456) to Charles Wilkins (1778).

Like the evolution of writing-materials from the stage of 'Papyrus' in and around Egypt to 'Palm-leaves' in and around the Indian subcontinent, till we reached the stage of 'Paper', the methods of printing also underwent a series of changes from the stage of moveable metal types to the era of typeless photo offset printing. The honour of first introducing the moveable metal types goes to Johann Gutenberg of Germany, who first printed his famous '42-line *Bible*' in Latin in 1456. Still now Gutenberg is regarded as the 'Founder of moveable types' and in that sense, he can claim the honour as the 'Founder of modern printing'.

Similarly, Charles Wilkins may be regarded as 'Gutenberg of Bengal', being the Founder of modern Bengali printing. The portion of Bengali text of N.B. Halhed's *A Grammar of the Bengal Language* (1778) was printed with the metal types first introduced by Charles Wilkins. But it is pertinent to remember that Wilkins was largely assisted by the famous Bengali blacksmith and 'ingenious artist' Panchanan Karmakar who had the rare credit of cutting the Bengali metal-types under the guidance of Wilkins. Eventually Panchanan's talent and natural skill in the art of metal cutting drew the attention of William Carey, founder of the Baptist Mission of Serampore, who engaged Panchanan in his pioneer Serampore Mission Press for cutting Bengali types for many of its Bengali publications issued on and from 1800, viz., Carey's *Dharmapustak* (1801)—a part of which under the title *Mangal*

Samachar Matiur Rachita was separately published in 1800, Ram Ram Bosu's *Raja Pratapaditya Charitra* (1801) and *Lipimala* (1801), Carey's *Kathopakathan* (1801), Goloknath Sharma's *Hitopadesh* (1802), Mrityunjoy Vidyalankar's *Batrish Sinhasan* (1802), Kashiram Das's *Mahabharat* (4 vols, in 1801-1803), Kirtibash's *Ramayana* (in 5 vols., in 1802-1803), etc. All these early publications strengthened the foundation of Bengali prose and widened the area of Bengali printing. With this modest beginning, Bengali printing has now reached a very advanced stage having world-class excellence in its various aspects.

Of course, Bengali printing is not an exception. The story of this advancement is equally true in case of printing throughout the world. The most striking feature about the advancement of book-printing that took place with the advancement of technology was that, it became possible to produce multiple copies, at a considerable higher speed and in far superior colourful presentation.

In course of evolution, book-production has undergone a sea-change, and ultimately we have now reached the stage of e-publication. The world of books had started to go digital. In the backdrop of current technological advancement, books are now making what may be called the biggest technological leap since Gutenberg invented moveable type in 1456. A recent news release in November 2008 from Paris highlights that a group of European libraries and archives plans to open 'Europeana', an online database of two million books and other historical items, including films, paintings, newspapers and sound recordings. The book business has also taken a new turn when the technology helps people publish their own books using Internet. In fine, the fantastic advancement of technology has brought sea-change in the field of book production as well as our libraries. It appears that our traditional concept of books and libraries is under serious threat, ominously suggesting their extinction in the coming days. But fortunately, people at large cannot afford to forego their pleasure of leisurely browsing at the brilliantly printed colourful books of their choice stored in public libraries where they can easily step in at their own time and alone be absorbed in self-study without any aid of hired equipments. Hence, printed books still survive and continue to grow in rapid pace, ensuring longevity and steady demand for public libraries.

But still the threat persists from some other corner which is no less an agency like the widely spread powerful electronic media, mostly the TVs. Tempting, colourful TV programmes may pose a new challenge to the world of books and the reading habits of the people. In view of this apparent conflict between 'book culture' and 'screen culture', we wonder whether the electronic text can replace the many forms of the printed codex-book, magazine, newspaper and so forth. The more likely reasonable, possibility is the coexistence of the two in the decades to come. That's the way we can face the new challenge and sustain and develop the book culture in the years to come.

Earlier prediction of death of cinema with the advent of TV has not been proved true. Hourly news from Radio and TV channels have so far failed to reduce the ever increasing newspaper sales. The evidence of decline in book production has also not been noticed anywhere in the world. Rather we hope, more and more innovative book productions will be developed to face the challenge of the day.

IV

Every art or technology, in course of its development, goes through a process of evolution. We have so far discussed about the evolution of books and printing. Similarly is equally interesting the history of evolution of libraries, particularly the public libraries in which we are more concerned in our present discourse. The basic driving force that characterised the evolution of libraries is the urge of the common people to have more and more access to the library and its collection. The history started when the books, rather the manuscripts were confined within the privileges of the priests or the monks only and the books were very often 'chained' within the Buddhist 'Bihars' or temples or churches. The situation changed a little when the books came under the control of the rich, the landlords or the kings. But still the common people were far from having any access to those prestige collections. But with the passing of time, gradually emerged libraries for the public in true sense, from which started the process of democratisation. Pubic libraries were freed from religious stranglehold or individual ownership and were bestowed with public custody and free access. The UNESCO Public Library Manifesto 1994 has defined the public library as the local centre of information, making all kinds of knowledge and information readily available to its users.

The arena of public library services are widening day by day in response to the growing needs of the users, mostly representing the common people at large. Community Information Service (CIS) has emerged as the new horizon of public library services and it now poses a challenge for the public library services in the new millennium. The unique characteristic of the CIS is that it serves the daily problem-solving needs of the downtrodden people who have no access to other sophisticated sources of information. Secondly it helps participation in the democratic process and thus can strengthen the foundation of democracy.

The experts agree that the CIS is provided to help people 'with daily problem solving or in raising the quality of their lives', and it services 'those who belong to the lower socio-economic group or are disadvantaged'. The Library Association of UK has explained CIS as – 'a positive decision.... to act either individually or collectively on their problems in the fields of housing, employment, family and personal matters, consumer affairs, household finance, education, welfare rights and civil rights'. A public library in the backdrop of this wider dimension is referred to as the 'poor man's university'.

V

Incidentally, we may recall the Nobel Laureate Prof. Amartya Sen's lecture on "Demands of Social Justice" which he delivered as the Prof. Hiren Mukherjee Memorial Parliamentary Lecture in the Central Hall of Parliament on 11th August, 2008. Prof. Sen said in his lecture: "Social activities are an integral part of the working of democracy which is not just about institutions, such as elections and votes".

These social activities among others include organising public libraries where people of all walks of life can have free access in search of knowledge, information and pleasure. Thus the public libraries can help the working of democracy in a big way.

Prof. Amartya Sen further said, "Indian democracy has been far less effective in dealing with problems of chronic deprivation and continuing inequity with adequate urgency, compared with extreme threats of famines and other emergencies".

One way of dealing with 'chronic deprivation' of our millions of downtrodden people would be to acknowledge their right to education or knowledge or information. And this acknowledgement may come in the way of providing them free community information service.

Before I conclude, I would like to make a reference to the Library Mission recently initiated by the National Knowledge Commission of India. I welcome it wishing its speedy implementation. The Commission while fully appreciating the emerging new role of the public libraries has said that 'Libraries have a recognised social function in making knowledge publicly available to all. They serve as local centres of information and learning, and are local gateways to national and global knowledge'.

The Prime Minister of India took the initiative to establish the National Knowledge Commission in 2005 with his commitment for the 'foundation of a knowledge economy'. It's now time for India to accept the 'challenge of making access to knowledge a reality for all'. Establishment of a network of millions of libraries with well-planned community information service can be the answer to the challenge.

3

Library Vision 2020

If we desire to cherish a vision, we must have a mission to successfully achieve it. Our library vision is a society of knowledge and information for all, our library mission is to build up a system that may enable all to reach there. We may thus set our library mission to successfully implement our library vision for the next decade. Library Vision 2020 is not far away from us. But it must have tremendous potential to change our present day library system befitting the needs of a fast changing society.

Incidentally we may refer to the voluminous IASLIC publication, titled 'Library Profession in search of a New Paradigm', containing papers submitted for the XXIII National Seminar of IASLIC (Indian Association of Special Libraries and Information Centres) held at Bose Institute, Kolkata in December 2008, wherein the editors have observed: 'Revolutionary developments in the field of ICT and their increasing applications in the field of library and information services have ushered in a new paradigm and its effect has been felt all over, India being no exception. The library and information profession in the country needs to quickly equip itself to meet the challenges of the new paradigm'.

They have thus set a challenging mission for the Library Profession in search of a new paradigm.

But perhaps it is confined within a specific area of specialised library profession. In order to identify a future library vision in general, we need to extend it far beyond the specialised field to take care of the needs of about 54,000 public libraries working in our country. These libraries are assigned to cater to the needs of a larger number of people whose literacy level and socio-economic status are neither so high nor so enviable as competent library user. Here lies the critical nature of our library development programme and we must design our library vision of a decade ahead keeping in view the limitations of receptivity of our prospective users, but at the same time the infinite needs of that hapless multitude of unsophisticated prospective users.

We are dreaming and planning of a library system in a society, with a population of about 121 crore, whose literacy has so far reached 74 per cent (as per 2011 Census) from the previous 64.8 per cent (as per 2001 Census), still leaving a quarter of our population illiterate, and whose national average of village electrification is 82.3 per cent (by February 2010), with nearing 20 per cent of villages yet to be electrified, and number of connections (as on 15.8.2011) to BPL households being only 68.8 per cent (i.e., 14% less than national average). Moreover, joblessness is about 8 per cent, with huge chronic under-employment, whereas percentage of people living below poverty line is 37.2 per cent (as per Tendulkar Committee report). Shockingly, there are still 1,21,653 habitations, which have some drinking water sources with quality problems, and a large section of population is still devoid of proper health-care facilities. In such a situation we are envisaging Library Vision 2020. We must, therefore, always keep in view the reality of the situation.

Meanwhile, we are at the end of the Eleventh Five Year Plan (2007 to 2012) and in the next year would cross the threshold of the Twelfth Five Year Plan (2012 to 2017). Moving further our Library Vision 2020 will be under the nourishing care of the thirteenth Five Year Plan (2017-2022). We may, therefore, reasonably hope that our 2020 Library Vision will have a better socio-economic situation to nurse our idealistic vision of a decade ahead. Still we need to ponder how much we can make progress in the intervening period.[1,2]

A remarkable change has, of course, already set in the arena of library movement with the advent of a new concept of

Knowledge Society and the establishment of the National Knowledge Commission under the Chairmanship of Dr. Sam Pitroda with effect from 2005. Working under the direct patronage of the Government of India, the Commission applauds its unique role with the claim that 'India seized the challenge of making access to knowledge 'a reality for all'. The Commission further states: "A library is not a building stacked with books—it is a repository and source of information and ideas, a place for learning and enquiry, and for the generation of thought and the creation of new knowledge. Public libraries in particular have the potential to bridge the gap between the 'information poor' and the 'information rich' by ensuring that people from all sectors and settings of society and the economy across India have easy access to knowledge they seek".

One aspect of our Library Vision 2020 may, therefore, aim to 'transform our present unequal knowledge society into an egalitarian, progressive knowledge society'.

It is claimed by the Knowledge Society that developments in Information & Communication Technology (ICT) have so far enabled libraries to provide wide public access to all, and to bridge the gap between the local, national and global levels. This may be interpreted as impact of globalisation.

It is, of course, felt by a group of library experts that the library and information services sector in India has not kept pace with the paradigmatic changes taking place in society. It is imperative that all libraries—public, academic, research and special—change gear and develop at an accelerated pace, as we envisage in our Library Vision 2020.

While discussing about 'Library Vision 2020', we may refer to a similar exercise made by a Committee [Committee on India Vision 2020] constituted by the Planning Commission of India in the year 2000, "as a part of the exercise on Tenth Plan (2002-2007) to develop a long-term twenty-year vision for helping to work out a medium-term programme for India's development strategy. The Committee took more than two years to have an integrated and consistent view of how the countrymen would like to see India in the year 2020". The Committee produced a Report titled *India: Vision 2020* (2004). [Arun Ghosh has referred to it in his paper included in the aforesaid IASLIC publication, 2008.]

One of the background papers included in this Report was on 'Towards Knowledge Society: Vision 2020', subscribed by Garry Jacobs and N. Asokan.

The authors began their Paper with the observation: "Imagine an India in which elementary school enrolment (I–VIII) and adult literacy are approaching 100 per cent, school dropout rates are nearly zero, all children who are not going on for higher academic studies receive vocational training and computer literacy are almost up to the standard of Western nations. Imagine a country in which nearly all citizens have access to all forms of print and electronic communication media—television, telephone, the internet.

"Compare that with India as it is today, with only 64 per cent of its people meeting even the most minimum standard of literacy, where 59 per cent of students never complete fifth standard, where secondary enrolment is 58 per cent… and where probable less than 1 per cent of the working age population is computer literate."

In the background of such dismal picture, we need to review the connotation of the term 'Knowledge Society', which in turn is an extension of another term 'Information Society'.

An expert in the subject, Andrew Whitworth observes: Information Society is a society in which information, rather than material goods, has become the chief economic, social and cultural motor. The implication is that it is the world's richer economies, principally in North America, Europe, Japan and Australia who are making or have already made this transition. The information society has been developing for some decades now—perhaps even centuries—and though new technologies have accelerated its evolution, the process is far from complete, particularly when considered globally (remember that over a billion people alive today have never made a telephone call). The information society's future will be shaped, to a large extent, by social, political and cultural factors that are less easy to predict or direct. [Ref. 'Information Society'. *International Encyclopaedia of Information and Library Sciences,* 2nd edn. 2003.]

Incidentally, we should make a note that National Knowledge Commission has been constituted with a big idea of achieving a knowledge society in our country. The Commission itself, while highlighting its important role that it is designed to perform states: "The Commission's overarching aim is to transform India into a vibrant knowledge-based society. This entails a radical improvement in existing systems of knowledge as well as the creation of avenues for generating new forms of knowledge. Increased participation and a more equitable access to knowledge across all sections of society are of vital importance in achieving these goals".

Public libraries can be the most effective vehicle to achieve this 'equitable access to knowledge'. This would be a major component of our Library Vision 2020.

The National Knowledge Commission thus sets the goal: 'The goal is to transform libraries from guarded storehouses of publications into open stockpiles of knowledge'. 'Libraries can assist in setting up facilities to preserve and give access to indigenous knowledge and the nation's cultural heritage'.

The NKC rightly reminds us: 'Libraries have a recognised social function in making knowledge publicly available to all. They serve as local centres of information and learning and are local gateways to national and global knowledge'.

This local centre of information, working through the local public library, renders the most valuable information service to its neighbouring community—commonly known as 'Community Information Service' (CIS) throughout the world. Since its introduction in the latter half of the last century in a small way in India, now appears to draw a bigger and essential demand by the poor and downtrodden people to improve the quality of their life. Since these hapless poor people have no other means of access to information (and knowledge) necessary for their 'daily problem solving', public libraries in their respective neighbouring localities can take the vital role of rendering the essential 'Community Information Service' (CIS) to them. We may dream of a situation by the end of next decade when every Panchayat or Municipality in our country will have one well equipped library to render most effective CIS to the people around. This can be another major component of our Library Vision 2020.

If we always think of an enlightened Knowledge Society wherein the libraries equipped with ICT are ready to serve the educated elite society, we cannot do justice to the entire populace of our society which is sharply divided among the 'haves' and 'have-nots'—both in the sense of socio-economic status and information-accessibility. To be precise, we cannot ignore the reality of this digital divide in our society.

There is a sharp divide between two groups of our citizens—one is 'online citizens', and the other who have no access to Internet services may be called "non-internet citizens". The fact remains that this second group of people constitutes the vast majority of our population who are generally poor and disadvantaged. This disparity has created the digital divide.

Interestingly, the "economic have-nots" status also makes them—in most cases—"information have-nots". This group of people constitute vast majority, about 85 per cent of our population. In our Library Vision 2020, we must think about these people and provide CIS to them through the entire public library system network established throughout the country. This can be one of the most effective approach to reverse the "digital divide" by reaching out to the "Information Have-nots".

A distinguished American Library Science expert Joseph C. Donohue has defined Community Information Service (CIS) as the 'Information needed to cope with crises in the lives of individuals and communities'. There are two types of information—one is 'Survival Information', which is related mainly with problems of Health, Housing, Earnings, Legal Safety, Financial aids and opportunities, Political rights, etc. The other type of information is 'Citizen Action Information', which is needed for participation in socio-political activities. The Library Association of U.K. has further elaborated the community information as "those, which assist individuals and groups with daily problem-solving and with participation in the democratic process. The CIS concentrate on the needs of those who do not have ready access to other sources of assistance and on the most important problems that people have to face, problems to do with their homes, their jobs and their rights".

CIS is further explained as—'a logical response to demonstrated need for non-book information about community resources'.

The basic object of CIS is to utilise the public libraries not only as the traditional repository of books and journals, but also as Library Resource Centres (LRC) enriched with valuable collections of Audio Visual Materials (AVM) and other Non-Book Materials (NBM) and information sources which can reach out to millions of poor illiterates, helping them in solving their numerous daily life problems and satisfying their needs, and demands for 'education, culture and information'. The Community Information Centres at the primary unit public libraries thus enlarge their users' base and in turn, strengthen our democratic foundation. Indeed CIS is now a challenge to us, and its successful implementation throughout the country by 2020 can only ensure fulfilment of our national target of developing countrywide network of public library services at the grassroots level. This is indeed a major component of our Library Vision 2020.

Two important bodies also corroborate this Library vision. First one is the UNESCO—, which has given us some radical new ideas on how to shape and channelise the public library services in the coming years. The 'UNESCO Public Library Manifesto' (1994), prepared in cooperation with the IFLA, has incorporated the following as the key missions of public libraries: 'ensuring access for citizens to all sorts of community information', 'providing adequate information services to the local enterprises, associations and interest groups'.

While proclaiming UNESCO's belief in the public library as a 'living force for education, culture and information', the Manifesto asserts that the 'public library is the local centre of information, making all kinds of knowledge and information readily available to its users'.

The second one, is the Committee set up by the Government of India under the Chairmanship of Prof. D.P. Chattopadhyay for formulating a National Policy on Library and Information System in India. The Committee in its report submitted in May 1986 emphasised the need to introduce community libraries in rural areas. It states—'a village or a village cluster with adequate population should have a community library, which will also serve as an information centre. Resources of different agencies engaged in the work of public health, adult education, local self-government and such others may be pooled to build up this composite centre'.

In our Library Vision 2020, we look forward to fulfil these recommendations from the two aforesaid bodies.

Based on growing public demand, Public library-based CIS is now very popular throughout the world, particularly in US, Canada, Australia, U.K. and other Western countries. As is practised abroad, the principal public library, along with its many branches located in different far and near places, provides CIS to its respective local areas. This CIS is a part of their total library service. By virtue of this additional CIS, those libraries are gradually becoming more and more popular and pro-people in nature. These are all, of course, online database information instantly provided through internet. But as an exception, the New York Public Library and all its branches, besides providing CIS through Internet, also maintain a special 'Community Information Service Collection' consisting of handbooks, guides, pamphlets and brochures.

In our country, while we are planning introduction of library-based CIS in a wider scale, we must keep in mind the model of New York Public Library, which maintains an additional printed 'CIS collection' for its users. This printed hard copy model will mostly suit our users. Information is now a commodity and that, too, is costly. Moreover, information technology is also not very commonly available in our wide-spread rural-based society. Above all, the have-nots or the poor-neglected exploited people for whom we are planning to provide CIS, do not have necessary facilities, or mind-set, and technical expertise or financial capabilities to avail of the computer or internet services. We, therefore, need to concentrate on collection of printed information booklets or handbooks. In view of our present socio-economic condition, this can be our proper approach. In our Library Vision 2020, we hope to have chain of such CIS centres along with the chain of public libraries connecting the people throughout the whole country.

Before I conclude, I respectfully remember our national poet Rabindranath Tagore in his 150th birth anniversary and recall with reverence how deeply he touched on the principal duty of the Libraries. Poet Tagore said, library puts the users on the crossing of thousands of ways, one can go on the way of his own choice, nobody will object. He further said, it is the principal duty of the library to facilitate the full acquaintance of the user with the book (information and knowledge) in a purposeful way. This message, I believe, can take care of all our efforts to successfully implement Library Vision 2020. All we need to realise, again as advocated by Poet Tagore—"*Purano sanchaya niye phire phire becha-kena ar chalibe na*"—We cannot go on marketing with our old stock, we must have new idea, new energy, new resource and new enterprise.

Notes

1. Incidentally, we can refer to relevant objective of the Twelfth Five Year Plan: "Recognising the growing use of technology in knowledge delivery, promotion of e-books and digitisation of National Book Trust (NBT) books and records will be taken up during the Twelfth Plan. Capacity of NBT would be strengthened to discharge its new responsibilities".

— *Twelfth Five Year Plan* (2012-2017), Vol. III, p. 110, published by Planning Commission, Government of India, New Delhi.

2. The Plan document further provides the growth data: "During the past 10 years, India's overall share of publication in the world has risen from 2.8 per cent to 3.4 per cent, with a significant improvement in researcher productivity since 1999. India produces over twice as many scientific publications a year than it did a decade ago. Though dwarfed by China's achievements, India's output of publications has grown faster than that of Brazil and Russia".

   — *Twelfth Five Year Plan* (2012-2017), Vol. III, p. 112, New Delhi.

4

Multi-Faceted Approach towards Development of Public Libraries in India

Expansion of Users Base

Whatever be the outcome of a National Policy, the basic fact is that the ultimate success of any public library system depends on the number of users coming forward to avail of the library services. In other words, the number of users appears to be the first criterion of effectiveness of any public library system. The more popular a public library will be, the more wider should be its users base. But in reality, we find a dismal picture if we make a survey of the users base of our public libraries. Generally, the membership strength of a public library may be taken as an indication of its users base. And when this membership strength is evaluated against the total population of the region served by the library, the real picture of the users base is revealed.

Users Survey

Various readership surveys, as regularly conducted in the U.K., U.S.A. or other Western countries, have revealed that the public libraries generally serve only one-quarter to one-third, i.e., 25 per cent to 33 per cent of the total population. Bernard Berelson in his famous study 'The library's public' (1949) identified that public libraries served only 15-25 per cent of the population in the U.K. The later surveys in the U.K. revealed that this coverage hardly went up to 33 per cent of the population. [Allan Bunch, 'Community information services'.—London: Clive Bingley, 1982.] In our country there has not been any such significant methodical survey of public library users. But on notional basis, it can be said that our readership coverage is in no way better if not worse in view of higher percentage of illiteracy in our country. One very disappointing picture has been revealed in a recent status report prepared by the Directorate of Library Services, West Bengal. The report has given districtwise number of government and sponsored libraries (1991-92) along with their total membership (adult and children) number, against the population figure (1991 Census) of each district. On an analysis of the report it is found that the total membership of all the government, and sponsored libraries of the State hardly covers one per cent (1%) of the total population of the State. [Dr. S.R. Ranganathan Birth Centenary Workshop on the Public Library System in West Bengal, 11th-13th September, 1992. Salt Lake, Calcutta: Working Papers.] It is really a matter of great concern for the public library situation in the country. The situation may be analysed from the other angle, when it may be noticed that the public library readers, by and large, cover only the middle class of the society. The upper class people generally find it below their status to come down to the public library to avail of its books or other services and on the other hand the lower socio-economic group of people generally, do not find any interest or leisure time, nor do they have requisite education or aptitude for public library use. As a result of such a situation, the majority of the population are kept out of the purview of the services and benefits of public libraries, despite the fact that these libraries are funded by public exchequer.

This appeared to be a sheer wastage of public money and public energy as well. The worldwide library profession as a whole became much concerned about such a situation and started thinking of a way out for effective utilisation of public library services. The obvious means was to expand the users base, which was in turn dependent on the library leaders' capability in creating public interest in library services.

Public Interest in Library Services

Thus the library organisers became primarily involved in creating public interest and attracting them towards libraries. Consequently, the concept of library services has also undergone a sea-change during the last few decades, both in Western countries as well as in Indian context.

Emerging New Concept of Library

The traditional idea of library as a storehouse of knowledge confined within the pages of printed books only is rather obsolete now-a-days, and obviously the librarian is also no more regarded as a mere keeper or custodian of books. Bidding farewell to the traditional custodian mentality, the librarian has to assume now-a-days the role of a social leader of the people around his neighbouring society with the key task of satisfying their needs and demands for information—may be for educational, cultural or leisure purposes. To achieve this social task the librarian has to collect, along with books, various other non-book materials which have proved to be essential tools for achieving his goal. Aided with these NBM tools the librarian can invite and attract the people to call on the library and then retrieve and present the desired information to his invitee clientele, many of whom are obviously illiterate, through various audio-visual formats and thereby giving them utmost satisfaction with a touch of pleasant surprise indeed.

Thus in a changing scenario, the public library is committed to satisfy the users' needs and demands for various informations. 'The library serves a community and provides the facilities for the retrieval of a variety of informations. Printed materials—books, periodicals, pamphlets—remain important carriers of that information, but complementary to them now are an increasing range of valuable non-book formats.' [Richard Fothergill & Ian Butchart, *Non-book Materials in Libraries: A Practical Guide*—London: Clive Bingley, 1978.]

Study of the Neighbouring Public

The other important aspect of this information service is the need to study the character of the neighbouring public—their socio-economic status, their educational background and their means of livelihood—and to assess whether the locality is rural or urban-based and/or agriculture or industry-based or predominantly an area of middle class service-holders, etc. Once we can determine this character of the potential user population, we may assess their information needs and accordingly, we may organise our library resources to satisfy their needs and demands. On the other hand, once we can get ourselves equipped with the necessary type of library materials, tools and methodology to satisfy the users' needs, our clientele will also start feeling interest in the libraries and will throng in increasing number in the library. The users' base will thus be automatically expanded.

Types of Public Library Services

Various types of library services, like information and referral service, community information service, audio-visual programmes, extension or outreach programmes, etc., can be offered to the public to attract them and to sustain their interest in libraries. And obviously these services include not only the traditional printed books, but rather a growing emphasis is given on various non-book information materials in accordance with the spirit of the proposed National Policy on Library and Information System in India.

National Policy on Library and Information System

The Committee on National Policy on Library and Information System under the Chairmanship of Prof. D.P. Chattopadhyay submitted a report in May 1986, emphasising on the need to introduce community libraries in rural areas. The relevant portion of the report may be reproduced here:

'The most important task before the Government is to establish, maintain and strengthen the free public libraries in the country and enable them to work as a system.

'The main thrust in this area should go to the rural public library. A village or a village cluster with an adequate population should have a community library which will also serve as an information centre. Resources of different agencies engaged in the work of public health, adult education, local self-government and such others may be pooled to build up this composite centre....

'The community library should also importantly cater for adult education and make adequate audio-visual aids available to attract the illiterate villagers....

'In addition to the usual services to be rendered by it (i.e., the district library), it should also provide for learning facilities and recreation for the handicapped. ...should provide literature in Braille. ...should also arrange mobile and circulating library services within its areas. ...Special services should be rendered to hospitals, prisons and the infirm in their homes...

'Libraries for special groups should be built in areas of tribal concentration or of minority communities to develop their distinctive cultures.'

UNESCO Recommendations for Public Libraries

'The UNESCO Public Library Manifesto 1972' may also be referred to in this context as a most valuable relevant document which recommends collection of NBM or AVM, along with books, in public libraries for developing education, culture and information services. Its relevant points are quoted below:

'The manifesto proclaims UNESCO's belief in the public library as a living force for education, culture and information.

> 'Since the printed word has been for centuries the accepted medium for the communication of knowledge, ideas and information, books, periodicals, newspapers remain the most important resources of public libraries.
> 'But science has created new forms of record and these will become an increasing part of the public library's stock, including print in reduced form for compact storage and transport, films, slides, gramophone records, audio and video tape, for adults and children, with the necessary equipment for individual use and for cultural activities.
> 'The public library is a natural cultural centre for the community, bringing together as it does people of similar interests. Space and equipment are, therefore, necessary for exhibitions, discussions, lectures, musical performances and films, both for adults and children.'

Introduction of Community Information Service

The Information and Referral (I&R) service is very often referred to as the Community Information Service (C.I.S.). An expert opinion explained it as 'a logical response to demonstrated need for non-book information about community resources'. [Clara S. Jones, (ed.), 'Public Library Information and Referral Service'. Gaylord Professional Publications, 1978.] With the emergence of new concept of public libraries and the changing scenario of public library services throughout the world, C.I.S. is increasingly gaining popularity, with the urge for its implementation at an early date. This trend started developing by the mid-sixties to mid-seventies of the present century.

Of course, it should always be kept in mind that this new information service is in no way going to replace the traditional book service, rather it has developed as complementary to the early book service.

What is meant by Community Information

While appreciating the need to develop CIS through our public libraries, we must clarify what is meant by community information. As the Library Association of the UK has a long tradition of introducing and developing CIS, we may take special note of their concept of community information. They have explained CIS as 'a positive decision to concentrate on enabling people, particularly those in lower socio-economic groups, to act either individually or collectively on their problems in the fields of housing, employment, family and personal matters, consumer affairs, household finance, education, welfare rights and civil rights'. For further clarification, Library Association has defined CIS as 'services which assist individuals and groups with daily problem-solving and with participation in the democratic process. The services concentrate on the needs of those, who do not have ready access to other sources of assistance and on the most important problems that people have to face, problems to do with their homes, their jobs and their rights'. [*Community Information: What Libraries Can Do: A Consultative Document.*— London: Library Association, 1980.]

Community Information Service—A Challenge to us

We need not feel shy in drawing lessons from the experiences of the Western countries where CIS have become an essential part of public library services since the mid-sixties. To be frank, the present status of our users service in public libraries is not very encouraging. In our efforts for improvement and expansion of this service, we must think of introducing CIS for the millions of poor illiterates who constitute the major part of our population. Perhaps it is better to look at them as 'unlettered', and not 'illiterate', who have keen sense of judgement, understanding and appreciation for new ideas. If we can provide them all the necessary information in their day-to-day problem-solving affairs through suitable non-book formats, i.e., the AV materials, they would very well receive them thankfully and be able to effectively utilise the resources available in the society.

Popularity and Wider User Base

Once the neighbouring community start enjoying the advantage of getting all the necessary information from the nearest library, they need not have to bother where to go for what information. Libraries will thus automatically become popular, with wider user base, and people will very often voluntarily step in the library with the prospect of gradually being attracted to the world of knowledge and recreation through books and non-book media. With the successful implementation of CIS our public libraries will also become, as a popular slogan once coined in Britain, 'A place to go when you don't know where to go'.

Improvement of Quality of Library Services

With the introduction of all these aforesaid suggested programmes and services, it may be possible to satisfy the present-day basic needs of improving the quality of public library services. This improvement should be in relation to depth and up-to-date information provided to the users, promptness and alertness to users' queries and sympathetic and helpful attitude towards the users. Unless we can improve this quality of library services, we cannot attract the users towards libraries.

Training of Library Personnel

For successful implementation of these suggested programmes and improvement of quality of library services, we need to introduce regular in-service training programmes for library personnel for upgrading their knowledge and expertise in modern library techniques and also for improving their attitude towards library service. It is expected that the Raja Rammohun Roy Library Foundation which functions as a promotional agency for public library development in India should take necessary initiatives and measures in this direction for comprehensive training of working public library personnel. We are hopeful to note the Foundation's reactions in this respect: 'The Foundation has recognised the fact that the content and quality of library service need regular evaluation and improvement with the changing needs of the society. To cater to this requirement the Foundation has adopted 'the scheme of assistance towards organisation of orientation or refresher training courses'. [*Books for the Millions at their Doorsteps*, p. 17.]

5

Library Services at the Grassroots Level

Public Libraries as Community Information Centres

Books on People, People for the Books

Even poet Rabindranath Tagore once regretted that he couldn't reach the people at all levels—particularly at the grassroots level. He wished he could echo the voices and aspirations of the people who were close to the earth, and could share the sentiments and realities of the lives of the peasants and the workers. This is, in general, the aspiration of all great poets and authors who look for portraying in their works the life at the grassroots level of the society, and their valuable works decorate the shelves of the rural public libraries. But the question remains, whether their works ultimately reach the target people at the grassroots level, or whether those downtrodden people can ever step in the libraries to browse at the pages of those invaluable works depicting their lives. In reality, there is a continuing wide gap between the printed books and their theme characters. In fact, public libraries are mostly middle class oriented. Upper class people generally think it below their status and prestige to call on the public libraries to avail of their services. On the other hand, people of lower socio-economic group generally do not have adequate leisure-time, nor any literary capability or appreciativeness to call on the public libraries to avail of their services. As a result of such readership imbalance, the readership base is narrowed down and the public money spent on the libraries is also not properly utilised.

Hence, the social leaders and public library experts started looking for alternative means to get rid of this imbalance plaguing such vital social institutions and to put them on right track for effective utilisation of their resources and widening their users' base. The ultimate result of such world-wide years long thinking is the Information and Referral Service, or more precisely, the Community Information Service (CIS).

Democratic Values of Community Information Service

The basic objects of the CIS is to utilise the public libraries not only as the traditional store-houses of books and journals, but also as Library Resource Centres (LRC) enriched with valuable collections of audio-visual materials (AVM) and other non-book materials (NBM) and information sources which can reach out to the millions of poor illiterates, helping them in solving their numerous daily life problems and satisfying their needs and demands for 'education, culture and information'. Such socially conscious LRCs constantly strive to attract the downtrodden to the centres or even they try to reach out to the physically handicapped or otherwise confined (in hospitals, prisons, etc.) people and millions of poor illiterate (rather say, 'unlettered' having keen sense of understanding) people through their various outreach programmes. In fact, they follow the famous axiom that when Mohammad cannot go to the mountain, the mountain itself comes down to Mohammad. The Community Information Centres at the primary unit public libraries thus enlarge their users' base and in turn, strengthen our democratic foundation. Indeed CIS is now a challenge to us, and its successful implementation throughout the country by the beginning of the twentyfirst century can only ensure fulfilment of our target of developing countrywide network of public library services at the grassroots level.

UNESCO Manifesto provides New Guidelines

Rightly representing the trend of world-thinking in this line, the UNESCO have also come forward with revolutionary new ideas on how to shape and channelise the public library services in the coming years. Such ideas are depicted in the latest version of their manifesto, viz., the 'UNESCO Public Library Manifesto, 1994'. The first edition of the Manifesto was published in 1949, while it incorporated some changes in its second edition published in 1972. But its 1994 version, prepared in cooperation with the IFLA (International Federation of Library Associations and Institutions), makes further changes incorporating quite a few new ideas to keep pace with the rapidly growing Information Technology (IT) and its scope for applications in public library services.

In relevance to our present study, it is particularly noted that the UNESCO Public Library Manifesto 1994 incorporates the following, along with others, as the key missions of public libraries:

- ensuring access for citizens to all sorts of community information;
- providing adequate information services to local enterprises, associations and interest groups; and
- supporting and participating in literacy activities and programmes for all age groups, and initiating such activities if necessary.

While proclaiming "UNESCO's belief in the public library as a living force for education, culture and information", the Manifesto asserts that the "public library is the local centre of information, making all kinds of knowledge and information readily available to its users". The Manifesto also emphasises that the public library must provide to "all age groups' materials relevant to their needs" and at the same time, "high quality and relevance to local needs and conditions are fundamental".

Thus the UNESCO Manifesto is very clear in its guideline that public libraries can be developed as community information centres for providing library and information services at the grassroots level.

Indian National Policy also provides Similar Guidelines

The Committee set up by the Government of India under the Chairmanship of Prof. D.P. Chattopadhyay for formulating a National Policy on Library and Information System in India submitted its report in May 1986. In its recommendations about our public library system, the Committee emphasised on the need to introduce community libraries in rural areas. The report states: "The most important task before the Government is to establish, maintain and strengthen the free public libraries in the country and enable them to work as a system. The main thrust in this area should go to the rural public library. A village or a village cluster with adequate population should have a community library which will also serve as an information centre. Resources of different agencies engaged in the work of public health, adult education, local self-government and such others may be pooled to build-up this composite centre".

Of course, even after decades we are still awaiting the policy implementation.

What Mooted the Concept of Such Composite Centre?

It took decades of many matured deliberations by social leaders and professional experts throughout the world to reach the conclusion that community information centres, composed of public libraries and information centres of various agencies, could be the best answer to popularise and widen the users' base of the rural public libraries and at the same time, to provide daily problem solving information needed by the millions of rural poors. In effect, it appears a very logical step to eliminate the multiplicity of information services rendered by various agencies and at the same time, it is a bold step to come out of the traditional idea of library and librarianship based on book-services only.

In Western countries, during the early days of developing outreach programmes in public libraries, community information was also seen as a means whereby the 'quality of life' could be raised. It helped unenterprising hapless poor to take initiatives and widen their sphere of activities to solve themselves their own problems. This self-help function is very much aligned with the public library ethos of individualised learning. Public library was, therefore, very rightly referred to as the "poor man's university". (Allan Bunch, *Community Information Services*, London: Clive Bingley, 1982.)

With the introduction of community information service, public library thus reached a very coveted position when it can offer something very helpful to the poor, who have no access to any other resources, and to the 'unlettered' who cannot read or write of his own, the hapless poor obviously then feel encouraged to regularly visit the community information centre where one day or other he may even feel interest in self-reading after availing of the centre's adult education and literacy programmes, CIS thus provides a unique opportunity for 'winning over the non-user to the joys of reading'. (Allan Bunch, *ibid.*, 'Information from the People to the People', by Arthur Curley: 'American Libraries", June 1979.)

In short, community information service is provided to help people 'with daily problem-solving or in raising the quality of their lives'; and it serves 'those who belong to the lower socio-economic groups or are disadvantaged'.

Introduction of Community Information—A Historical Perspective

Before we may further clarify the meaning of CIS and examine its various types and process of implementation, we may trace back the roots of its origin to ascertain the historical reasons for emergence of community information centres. Allan Bunch in his book on CIS has elaborately dealt with the subject. There is no denying of the fact that CI centres, may be of indifferent names, originated in Western countries, particularly in Britain and the United States, by the end of the nineteenth century. But its most significant development took place during the crisis period of the Second World War. In Britain Citizens' Advice Bureaux (CABx) were set up on emergency basis mainly to tackle various war oriented social problems, such as search for missing relations, evacuation and separation of family members, notification of emergency regulations, etc. With the outbreak of war time hostilities, people become crazy for all such information and the CABx played an important role to tackle the situation. Many public libraries were also then asked to open such information centres. But interestingly even after the end of war crisis CABx continued to play its role, rather with more vigour on public demand, in the field of personal and family problems not associated with the war. Eventually, with the emergence of new concept of library and librarianship, the work of CABx was taken over by CI centres in public libraries.

In the United States, Veterans' Information Centres, modelled on the CABx, were set up by the end of Second World War to deal with crises faced by men returning from the front to their communities who were then disparately needing information and advice regarding their rehabilitation and retraining programmes. Of course, with the setting down of the crises within a couple of years, most of these centres, totalling over 3,000 were closed by 1949.

But the people who once tasted the importance of such social information service urged for setting up CI centres. From the late sixties to early seventies started the present phase of development of CIS. 'Alienated' modern society, utterly lacking communication even between neighbours, pressed for the need for CIS. 'Society has become so complex that the experience of friends and neighbours is no longer enough. Specialist knowledge and skills are needed to cope with are increasingly forbidding bureaucratic apparatus'. In view of social needs library leaders came forward, from the seventies onwards, to introduce CIS into public libraries. 'By and large, the introduction of such services has been an act of faith by librarians committed to the idea'. (Allan Bunch, *ibid.*)

Thomas W. Shaughnessy concludes: 'our experience in trying to reach the disadvantaged, the urban and rural poor, taught us that in many instances books are not enough... what is so often needed is information, especially information on how to make bureaucracy work for the individuals and groups it is supposed to serve (*Information and Referral Service: Background and Issues*, by Thomas W. Shaughnessy).

CIS – A New Dimension of Public Library Service

Thus in a changing scenario, the public library is committed to satisfy the user community's needs and demands for various information. The public library is, therefore, now developed as a Library Resource Centre (LRC) being equipped with various information booklets and other NBM and AVM. Its service patterns may be graphically represented as follows:

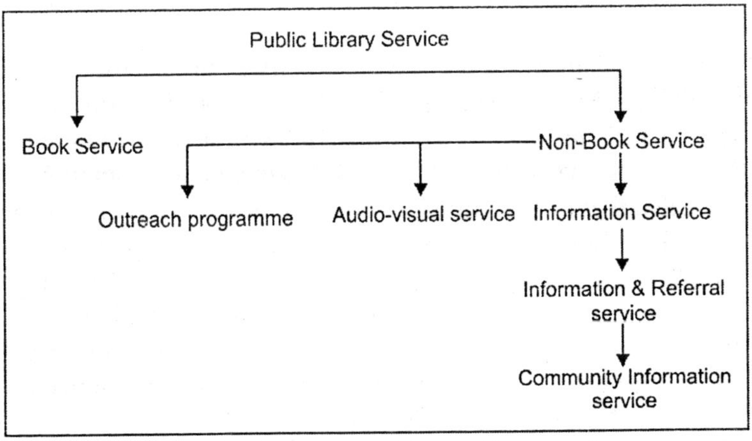

Fig. 5.1: Service Patterns of Public Library Service

To explain it precisely, public library on LRC's services may be broadly classified into two main needs—one is the traditional book service and the other is the newly developed non-book service. Among the non-book services are generally included the outreach programme (as is previously termed the Extension Programme). Audio-visual service and Information service). The information service is specified as the Information and Referral Service (I&RS) as the expert professional staff, who are trained in the related skills of using reference books and collecting, organising and disseminating non-book information, also very often refer the enquiries to appropriate sources for further help, with the advancement of IT (Information Technology), the smallest neighbourhood branch unit can now be linked in a network of information to other local, regional and national organisations. This I&R service is now-a-days very often broadly referred to as the CIS providing daily problem solving information to all the poor, and even illiterate members of the local community.

In view of the needs and demands for information by the downtrodden people of the society and with the emergence of new concept of public library service, which is no longer dependent on book service only, CIS is now gaining more and more popularity throughout the world, and, obviously, India cannot remain dissociated with this changing scenario. In fact, this has, of late, emerged as a challenge to us, particularly in view of the fact that India's adult literacy[1] rate is still very poor. A recent UN report (UNDP – Human Development Report 1995) revealed that in 1992 India's Adult Literacy rate was only 52 per cent, i.e., about 48 per cent of our adult population was illiterate. Even after five years, the position has not changed appreciably. In such a dismal situation, successful implementation of CIS through our grassroots level public libraries would indeed help us to strengthen the democratic foundation of our country.

What is meant by Community Information Service?

We must, at this stage, further clarify what is precisely meant by CIS. An expert opinion has explained the CIS as 'a logical response to demonstrated need for non-book information about community resources'. (Clara S. Jones, (ed.), *Public Library Information & Referral Service*, Gaylord Professional Publications, 1978).

While distinguishing CIS from two other similar terms, viz., 'Public Information' and 'Local Information', the Library Association of UK has explained CIS as 'a positive decision to concentrate to enabling people particularly these in lower socio-economic groups, to act either individually or collectively on their problems in the fields of housing, employment, family and personal matters, consumer affairs, household finance, education, welfare rights and civil rights. For further clarification, Library Association has defined CIS as 'services which assist individuals and groups with daily problems solving and with participation in the democratic process. The services concentrate on the needs of those who do not have ready access to other sources of assistance and on the most important problems that people have to face, problems to do with their homes, their jobs and their rights'. (*Community Information: What Libraries can do: A Consultative Document* – London: Library Association.)

Types of Community Information and their Helpful Use

As social being, people have various types of information queries in relation to their problems and needs of day-to-day life. It is the duty of the public librarian to meticulously collect and supply the necessary information booklets to satisfy such queries to their clientele as and when they call on him for the purpose. CI may cover a very wide field of our day-to-day needs, e.g., information on housing cooperative/bank loans financial assistance for various social projects, self-employment schemes, employment opportunities, locating and facilities of rural/agricultural banks, prices and availability—sources of various agricultural inputs (like seed, fertiliser, insecticide, oil and pump set, tractor, etc.) and also fishery and cottage or small-scale industry inputs, seed/soil testing centres, local markets and their products, scope for vocational training for their young wards, adult education provisions, family planning—hospital, medicare services, panchayat and cooperative self-help groups rules and facilities, legal aids, recent land reforms/tax law, amendments, savings schemes, sports and tourism and so on.

Current supporting booklets on such varied information should be judiciously collected in CI centres. Even collection of almanacs (*Panji*), bus and train timetables, road maps, etc., may prove to be of immense help to the local community.

Public libraries can work as organised resource centres where all the agencies involved in public welfare may be asked to go on supplying regularly and religiously all their up-to-date information brochures and publicity materials for proper dissemination of information to the people calling on libraries for aforesaid enquiries.

Trained library staff can extend the professional assistance to community groups in the work of acquisition and cataloguing classification—indexing of information materials and obviously, prompt dissemination of these information to the intending users. The CI centres can also be profitably utilised for post-literacy drive for the growing number of neo-literates.

Manual of Community Information Service

Once we decide to introduce CIS in our public libraries, we should prepare a manual of CIS incorporating therein a list of all the possible types and varieties of information queries and services that can be offered to users and also a compiled list of available current information booklet that can answer such queries.

This manual can best be compiled based on opinion survey of our target users, group discussions among librarians, joint discussions between authorities of public libraries and other government agencies and a survey of the publicity and information materials produced by different agencies, like central and different State government ministries, departments, directorates and research bodies. Once such a manual is prepared, copies of it can be supplied to different public libraries and librarians themselves will be free to make choice from it of the information services that they would like to offer to their clientele befitting the particular needs of the locality and collect accordingly the supporting information booklets published by different government and research bodies.

Model Town and Rural Library for Introduction of CIS

It is high time now for the library directorates of all the States where Public Library Act has already been introduced, with assistance of Raja Rammohun Roy Library Foundation to implement the CIS scheme, at least to start it on an experimental basis. Taking lessons from the experience of such introductory CIS and critically reviewing the areas of their success or shortcomings, full-fledged CIS can be introduced in the second phase in all the public libraries of the States. With the beginning of the twentyfirst century we can thus extend our public library services to the grassroots levels.

Quality of Service must of course Improve

The users cannot be satisfied if the quality of services is not improved. The information that is supplied must be accurate, detailed and up-to-date, and at the same time, the Reference Librarian must be prompt and alert, with helpful and sympathetic attitude towards this clientele. Adequate arrangements must also be made to ensure that all sorts of information may be available under one roof. Let us hope that with the cooperation of all agencies and library professionals, we would soon be able to reach such an ideal situation, when people will feel free to come to CI centres and neighbours will not have unnecessary speculations as to why he is going to CI centre (as very often happens when one goes to divorce-consultants or loan-centres).

CIS Guarantees Popularity and Wider user base for Public Libraries

Once the neighbouring community starts enjoying the advantage of getting all the necessary information from the nearest library-

cum-CI centre, they need not have to bother where to go for what information. Unlike other agency offices, extended library hours during evenings and weekends can also encourage people to attend it. Libraries will thus automatically become popular, with wider user base, and people will very often voluntarily step in the library with the prospect of gradually being attracted to the world of knowledge and recreation through book and non-book media. With the successful implementation of CIS our public libraries will also become, as a popular slogan once coined in Britain, 'a place to go when you do not know where to go'.

Note

1 As per Census 2001, literacy in net terms has recorded a hike of 13.17 per cent from 52.21 per cent in 1991 to 65.38 per cent in 2001, (*Hindustan Times*, New Delhi, 27-3-2001).

References

Allen Bunch, *Community Information Services*, London: Clive Bingley, 1982.

Arthur Curlay, 'Information from the people to the people', *American Libraries*, June 1979.

Clara S. Jones, ed., *Public Library Information and Referral Service*. Gaylord Professional Publications, 1978.

Community Information — What Librarian's can do?: A Consultative Document, London Library Association.

Thomas W. Shaughnessy, *Information and Referral Services: Background and Issues*.

6

Community Information Service

The Challenge of the Day

New Concept of Library and Librarianship

Public Libraries may offer their services in two ways: (1) through the delivery of book services, and (2) the other, through the introduction of Information and Referral services, which are often termed as Community Information Services.

Book service is the most traditional service offered by the libraries. In fact, libraries were traditionally regarded as the storehouse of knowledge confined within the pages of printed books and the librarian was supposed to be the keeper or custodian of those books. But of late this traditional concept of 'library' and 'librarianship' as well, has undergone a sea change giving rise to foundation of 'library resource centres' which collect not only the printed books, but also various types of non-book, materials, and arrange for retrieval of information stored therein for satisfying the needs of the new group of users that have emerged during the last two decades.

Thus, through a process of historical development public libraries have been urged to be equipped with new set of tools and resource materials for offering information and referral services to their users to satisfy their needs or demands for information—may be for educational, economic, cultural or recreational purposes.

Introduction of Community Information Service

This I&R service is very often referred to as the Community Information Service. An expert opinion explained it as 'a logical response to demonstrated need for non-book information about community resources'. [Clara S. Jones (ed.), *Public Library Information and Referral Service*. Gaylord Professional Publications, 1978.] With the emergence of new concept of public libraries and the changing scenario of public library services throughout the world, CIS is increasingly gaining popularity and urge for implementation at an early date. This trend started developing by the mid-sixties to mid-seventies of last century.

There are obvious reasons behind this new orientation of public library services and development of this new trend of CIS. Of course, it should always be kept in mind that this new information service is in no way going to replace, the traditional book service, rather it has developed as complementary to the earlier book service.

Readership Survey Identifies its Coverage and Character

Various readership surveys, as particularly conducted in the Western countries, have revealed that the readership base of the public libraries is generally confined within 25 per cent to 33 per cent of the total population. Bernard Berelson in his famous study *The Library's Public* (1949) identified that public libraries served only 15-25 per cent of the population in the UK. The later surveys in the UK revealed that this coverage hardly went up to 33 per cent of the population. [Allan Bunch, *Community Information Services*. London: Clive Bingley, 1982.] In our country, there has not been any such methodical survey of public library readership. But on notional basis, it can be said that our readership coverage is in no way better, if not worse, in view of higher percentage of illiteracy in our country. The other characteristic of this readership base is that the majority of the readers of public libraries by and large represent the middle class of the society. The upper class people generally think it below their status and prestige to come to the public library to avail of its books and services, while the lower socio-economic group of people generally has no interest, nor any leisure time or literary capability or appreciative aptitude for public library use. As a result of such a situation, the majority of the population are kept out of the purview of the services and benefits of public libraries, despite the fact that these libraries are funded from public exchequer. By the sixties to seventies of the last century, social leaders gradually became concerned about disproportionate growth of library user's base and hence concerted attempts were made to expand it to reach the poor comprising the majority section of the society. Among many other measures, CIS was one major outcome of these attempts during the last few decades.

Situation in India

But this development was mainly noticed in the Western countries. We, in India, are still lagging behind in this respect. When the public libraries are funded by taxpayers' money, we have moral obligation to extend their services and benefits to a larger section of population which is mostly illiterate and rural based in our country. This can be achieved through various measures, like introduction of library extension work or, as more precisely termed, outreach programmes, with the aid of non-book material like audio-visual materials and others. Introduction of Community Information Service is only another form of this programme for expanding our library users base. Of late, this has emerged as a challenge to us. Successful implementation of CIS through public libraries would indeed help us to strengthen the democratic foundation of our country.

Our National Policy also Aims at Developing CIS

The committee set up by the Government of India under the chairmanship of Prof. D.P. Chattopadhyay for the formulation of a National Policy on Library & Information System in India submitted its report in 1986. In its recommendations, among others, about our Public Library System, the Committee states: "The most important task before the Government is to establish, maintain and strengthen the free public libraries in the country and enable them to work as a system. The main thrust in this area should go to the rural public library. A village or a village cluster with an adequate population should have a community library which will also serve as an information centre. Resources of different agencies engaged in the work of public health, adult education, local self-government and such others may be pooled to build up this composite centre".

What is meant by Community Information?

While appreciating the need to develop CIS through our public libraries, we must clarify what is meant by community information? As the Library Association of UK has long tradition of introducing and developing CIS, we may take special note of their concept of community information. While distinguishing it from two other similar terms, viz., 'Public Information and 'Local Information', they have explained CIS as 'a positive decision to concentrate on enabling people, particularly those in lower socio-economic groups, to act either individually or collectively on their problems in the fields of housing, employment, family and personal matters, consumer affairs, household finance, education, welfare rights and civil rights'. Of course, it is admitted that in spite of wide and fashionable application of the term CI, its use has become extremely confused. Hence, for further clarification, Library Association has defined CIS as 'services which assist individuals and groups with daily problem-solving and with participation in the democratic process. The services concentrate on the needs of those who do not have ready access to other sources of assistance and on the most important problems that people have to face problems to do with their homes, their jobs and their rights'. [Community Information: *What Libraries can do: A Consultative Document*, London: Library Association, 1980.]

Poor Man's University

In western countries, during the early days of developing outreach programmes in public libraries, community information was also seen as a means whereby the "quality of life" could be raised. It should allow people to extend themselves, take initiatives, broaden their sphere of competence, be enterprising. This self-help function is very much aligned with the public library ethos of individualised learning. There was a time in the early days of the movement when the public library was referred to as the "poor man's university". May be, community information services should be seen as a rediscovery, by the public library of its roots. [Allan Bunch, *ibid.*]

In short, community information is provided to help people 'with daily problem solving or in raising the quality of their lives', and it serves 'those who belong to the lower socio-economic groups or are disadvantaged'.

CIS — A Challenge to us

We need not feel shy in drawing lessons from the experiences of the Western countries where CIS have become an essential part of public library services since the mid-sixties. To be frank, the present status of our users' service in public libraries is not very encouraging at all. In our efforts for improvement and expansion of this service, we must think of introducing CIS for the millions of poor illiterates who constitute the major part of our population. Perhaps, it is better to look at them as 'unlettered', and not 'illiterate', who have keen sense of judgement, understanding and appreciation for new ideas. If we can provide them all the necessary information in their day-to-day problem-solving affairs through suitable non-book formats, i.e., the audio-visual materials, they would very well receive them thankfully and be able to effectively utilise the resources available in the society. 'Our experiences have taught us that in many instances books are not enough, 'what is so often needed is information, especially information on how to make bureaucracy work for the individuals and groups it is supposed to serve'. [Thomas W. Shaughnessy, *Information and Referral Services: Background and Issues*; Allan Bunch, *ibid.*]

Types and Patterns of Community Information

Public libraries can work as organised resource centres where all the agencies involved in public welfare may go on supplying regularly and religiously, all their up-to-date information brochures and publicity materials for proper dissemination of information to the people calling on the libraries for such enquiries. Trained library staff can extend the professional assistance to community groups in the work of acquisition of materials, cataloguing-classification-indexing of information materials and obviously, prompt dissemination of those information to their users as and when asked for.

CI may cover a very wide field of our day-to-day needs; e.g., information on housing and other cooperative society/bank loan systems, self-employment schemes, location and facilities of rural banks, prices and availability of various agricultural inputs and also fishery and cottage or small-scale industry inputs, local market for their products, scope for primary, secondary or vocational education for their young wards, Panchayat and Cooperative Society facilities, legal aids, tax laws, adult education provisions, tourism facilities, hospital services and so on. Even collection of almanacs ("*Panji*"), bus and train time-tables, weather bulletins, road maps, etc., may prove to be of immense help to the local community.

Manual of Community Information Services

Once we decide to introduce CIS in our public libraries, we should prepare a manual of CIS incorporating therein all the possible types and varieties of information services that can be offered to the users. This manual can best be compiled based on opinion survey of our target users, group discussions among librarians, joint discussions between authorities of public libraries and other government agencies and a survey of the publicity and information materials produced by different agencies. Once such a manual is prepared, copies of it can be supplied to different public libraries and librarians themselves will be free to make choice from it of the information services that they would like to offer to their clientele befitting the needs of the locality.

Library-Agency Cooperation

The suggestion of Library Association, UK is worth considering in this respect:

- "At the simplest level libraries can help agencies to publicise themselves in a number of ways—
  - by arranging special displays in library buildings featuring the work of different agencies;
  - by permanently displaying posters and leaflets in libraries to advertise services of agencies; and
  - by producing leaflets, posters and packs of materials, aimed at the public, to promote local advice agencies."

Advantages of CI Centre in Public Libraries

There are several advantages of organising community information centres in public libraries, viz.:

- expertise for organising information materials and handling queries are available with the professional staff;
- with the cooperation of all agencies, necessary supporting documents may be available in one place;
- wastage and expenses on running parallel agencies may be minimised, with the maximum utilisation of resources;
- all sorts of information may be available under one roof;
- reliability and credibility of library professionals; and
- people will feel free to come to CI centres and neighbours will not have unnecessary speculations as to why he is going to CI centre.

Popularity and Wider User Base

Once the neighbouring community starts enjoying the advantage of getting all the necessary information from the nearest library, they need not have to bother where to go for what information. Libraries will thus automatically become popular, with wider user base, and people will very often voluntarily step in the library with the prospect of gradually being attracted to the world of knowledge and recreation through book and non-book media. With the successful implementation of CIS our public libraries will also become, as a popular slogan once coined in Britain, 'A place to go when you don't know where to go'.

Towards Improvement and Expansion of Users Service

If our public libraries can provide increasing number and types of community information, which are mostly needed in day-to-day life of a modern complex society, more and more people, common poor people of lower socio-economic group having no access to other sources and agencies, will be attracted towards public libraries and thus their users base will be expanded and this would indeed be one very good way of improvement and expansion of users service in our public libraries.

7

Community Information Service

A Challenge for the Public Library Services in the New Millennium

No Further Business with the Old Stock

In the new millennium, it is high time for the exponents of public library services to realise that no further meaningful business can be continued merely with the stock of old commodities. Rabindranath Tagore has very nicely given a poetic expression to the idea. Poet Tagore urged people to move forward with new ideas towards the goal of a new destiny. CIS offers such a new dimension for public library services to satisfy the needs of the common people of the locality in a changing environment. CIS is based on a new idea—possibility of departure from the traditional idea of library services based on supply of books only—and in the backdrop of present-day decaying trend of readership in public libraries—promises to offer a novel opportunity for the library organisers to attract more and more people to the premises of the library and satisfy the users' multi-faceted daily information needs of life. With the buzzing of such newly attracted library users, our age-long decaying public libraries with only a handful of fiction-lovers, will get a fresh lease of life and develop into lively socio-cultural public institution.

Readership Imbalance Causes Narrow User Base

The problem may also be looked from a different angle. It is generally observed that public libraries are mostly middle class oriented. Upper class people generally think it below their status prestige to call on the public libraries to avail of their services. On the other hand, people of lower socio-economic group generally do not have adequate leisure-time, nor any literary capability appreciativeness to call on the public libraries to avail of their services. As a result of such readership imbalance, the user base is narrowed down.

Fall in User Base concerns Library Leaders

Occasional readership surveys in Western countries reveal that about 15 per cent to 25 per cent, and sometimes even up to 33 per cent, of the neighbouring population are covered by the public library service. Whereas, we have not yet been able to develop any such systematic survey in our country. But a preliminary estimate on West Bengal in the nineties, and our national estimate too, indicates that readership coverage here is hardly 1 per cent of the neighbouring population. Library leaders are quite very concerned about it and the public money spent on our public libraries cannot, therefore, be justified in our social context.

Hence, the social leaders and public library experts started looking for alternative means to get rid of this imbalance plaguing such vital social institutions and to put them in right track for effective utilisation of their resources and widening their users' base. The ultimate result of such worldwide years-long thinking is the Information & Referral Service, or more precisely, the CIS—the Community Information Service.

Democratic Values of Community Information Service

The basic objects of the CIS is to utilise the public libraries not only as the traditional repository of books and journals, but also as Library Resource Centres (LRC) enriched with valuable collections of audio-visual materials (AVM) and other non-book materials (NBM) and information sources which can reach out to the millions of poor illiterates, helping them in solving their numerous daily life problems and satisfying their needs and demands for 'education, culture and information'. The Community Information Centres at the primary unit public libraries thus enlarge their users' base and in turn, strengthen our democratic foundation. Indeed CIS is now a challenge to us, and its successful implementation throughout the country by the beginning of the twentyfirst century can only ensure fulfilment of our target of developing countrywide network of public library services at the grass roots level.

UNESCO Manifesto provides New Guidelines

Rightly representing the trend of world thinking in this line, the UNESCO have also come forward with revolutionary new ideas on how to shape and channelise the public library services in the coming years. Such ideas are depicted in the latest version (third edition) of their manifesto, viz., The 'UNESCO Public Library Manifesto 1994', prepared in cooperation with the IFLA, which incorporates the following along with others, as the key missions of public libraries:

- 'ensuring access for citizens to all sorts of community information; and
- providing adequate information services to the local enterprises, associations and interest groups'.

While proclaiming 'UNESCO's belief in the public library as a 'living force for education, culture and information', the Manifesto asserts that 'the public library is the local centre of information, making all kinds of knowledge and information readily available to its users'. The Manifesto also emphasises that the public library must provide to 'all age groups' materials relevant to their needs and at the same time, 'high quality and relevance to local needs or conditions are fundamental'.

Draft Indian National Policy also provides Similar Guidelines

The Committee set up by the Government of India under the Chairmanship of Prof. D.P. Chattopadhyay for formulating a National Policy on Library and Information System in India submitted its report in May 1986. In its recommendations about our public library system, the Committee emphasised on the need to introduce community libraries in rural areas. It states—"A village or a village cluster with adequate population should have a community library which will also serve as an information centre. Resources of different agencies engaged in the work of public health, adult education, local self-government and such others may be pooled to build up this composite centre".

Of course, even after decades, we are still awaiting a policy declaration and its implementation.

What mooted the Concept of such Composite Centre

It took decades of many matured deliberations by social leaders and professional experts throughout the world to reach the conclusion that community information centres composed of public libraries and information centres of various agencies, could be the best answer to popularise and widen the users' base of the rural public libraries and at the same time, to provide daily problem solving information needed by the millions of rural poor. In effect, it appears a very logical step to eliminate the multiplicity of information services rendered by various agencies and at the same time, it is a bold step to come out of the traditional idea of library and librarianship based on book-services only.

In Western countries, during the early days of developing outreach programmes in public libraries, community information was also seen as a means whereby the 'quality of life' could be raised. It helped unenterprising hapless poor to take initiatives and widen their sphere of activities to solve themselves their own problems. This self-help function is very much aligned with the public library ethos of individualised learning. Public library was, therefore, very rightly referred to as the 'poor man's university'. [Allen Bunch, *Community Information Services*. London: Clive Bingley, 1982.]

With the introduction of CIS, public library thus reached a very coveted position where it can offer something very helpful to the poor, who have no access to any other resources, and to the 'unlettered who cannot read or write of his own, the hapless poor obviously then feel encouraged to regularly visit the community information centre where one day or other he may even feel interest in self-reading after availing of the centre's adult education and literacy programmes. CIS thus provides a unique opportunity for 'winning over the non-user to the joys of reading'. [Allen Bunch, *ibid*.; 'Information from the people to the people', by Arthur Curlay: *American Libraries*, June 1979.]

The Essence of CIS

In short, community information service is provided to help people 'with daily problem-solving or in raising the quality of their lives'; and its services to 'those who belong to the lower socio-economic group or are disadvantaged'.

Introduction of Community Information—A Historical Perspective

There is no denying of the fact that CI centres, may be in different names, originated in western countries, particularly in Britain and the United States, by the end of nineteenth century. But its most significant development took place during the crisis period of the Second World War. In Britain Citizens Advice Bureaux (CABx) were set up on emergency basis mainly to tackle various war oriented social problems, such as search for missing relations, evaluation and separation of family members, notification of emergency regulations, etc. Many public libraries were also then asked to open such information centres. But interestingly even after the end of war crisis CABx continued to play its role, rather with more vigour on public demand; in the field of personal and family problems not associated with the war. Eventually, with the emergence of new concept of library and librarianship, the work of CABx was taken over by CI centres in public libraries.

In the United States, Veterans' Information Centres, modelled on the CABx, were set up by the end of Second World War to deal with crisis faced by men returning from the front to their communities who were then desperately needing information and advice regarding their rehabilitation. Of course, with the setting down of the crises within a couple of years, most of these centres, totalling over 3,000, were closed by 1949. But the people who once tasted the importance of such social information service urged for setting up CI Centres. From the late sixties to early seventies started the present phase of development of CIS. In view of various social needs library leaders came forward, from the seventies onwards, to introduce CIS into public libraries. 'By and large, the introduction of such services has been an act of faith by librarians committed to the idea'. [Allan Bunch, *ibid.*]

CIS—A New Dimension of Public Library Service

Thus in a changing scenario, the public library is committed to satisfy the user community's needs and demands for various information. The public library is, therefore, now developed as a Library Resource Centre (LRC) being equipped with various information booklets and other NBM and AVM.

The Information service, as mentioned above, is further specified as the Information and Referral Service (I & RS) as the expert professional staff, who are trained in the related skills of using reference books and collecting, organising and disseminating non-book information, also very often refer the enquirers to appropriate sources for further help, with the advancement of IT (Information Technology), the smallest neighbourhood branch unit can now be linked in a network of information to other local, regional and national organisation. This I & R service is now-a-days very often briefly referred to as

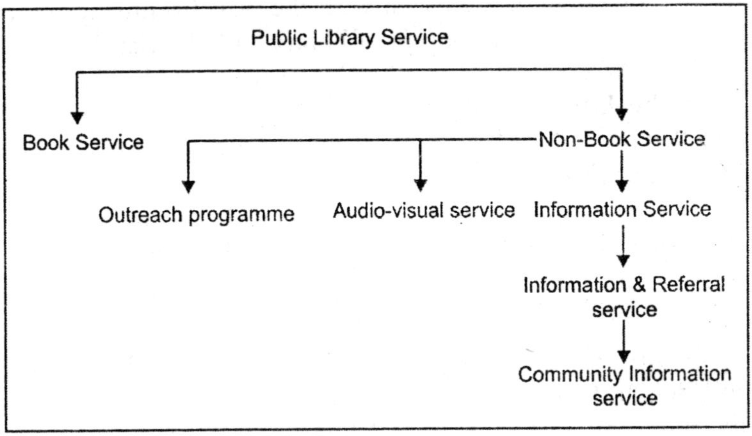

Fig. 7.1: Service Patterns

the CIS providing daily problem solving information to all the poor, and even illiterate, members of the local community.

In view of needs and demands for information by the downtrodden people of the society and with the emergence of new concept of public library service, which is no longer dependent on book service only, CIS is now gaining more and more popularity throughout the world, and, obviously, India cannot remain dissociated with this changing scenario. In fact, this has, of late, emerged as a challenge to us, particularly in view of the fact that India's adult literacy rate is still very poor. In such a situation, successful implementation of CIS through our grass roots level public librarians would indeed help us to strengthen the democratic foundation of our country.

What is Meant by CIS?

We further clarify what is precisely meant by CIS. An expert opinion explains it as—'a logical response to demonstrated need for non-book information about community resources'. [Clara S. Jones, (ed.), *Public Library Information & Referral Service*. Gaylord Professional Publication, 1978.]

The Library Association of UK has explained CIS as—'a

positive decision to concentrate on enabling people particularly those in lower socio-economic groups, to act either individually or collecting on their problems in the fields of housing, employment, family and personal matters, consumer affairs, household finance, education, welfare rights and civil rights'. [*Community Information: What Libraries can do—A Consultative Document*. London: Library Association, 1980.]

Type of Community Information and their Helpful Use

As social being, people have various types of information queries in relation to their problems and needs of day-to-day life. It is the duty of the public librarian to meticulously collect and supply the necessary information booklets to satisfy such queries to their clientele as and when they call on him for the purpose. CI may cover a very wide field of our day-to-day needs, e.g., information on housing co-operative/bank loans, financial assistance for various social projects, self-employment schemes, employment opportunities, location and facilities of rural/agricultural banks, prices and availability, sources of various agricultural inputs (like seeds, fertilisers, insecticides, oil and pump sets, tractors etc.) and also fishery and cottage and small scale industry inputs, seed/soil testing centres, local markets and their products, vocational training for their wards, adult education provisions, family planning/hospital/medicare services, panchayat and co-operative, self-help group rules and facilities, legal aids, recent land reform/tax law amendments, saving schemes, sports and tourism, and so on. Of late, information about the Central and State governments' current social welfare schemes, viz., 'Swarnajayanti' self-employment scheme, 'Annapurna' scheme, 'Sampurna' rural employment scheme, old-age and widow pension scheme, rural drinking water project, Pradhan Mantri Gram Sadak Yojana, Indira Awaas Yojana, National Rural Drinking Water Programme, etc., appear to be of vital importance to rural poor. Current supporting booklets on such varied information should be judiciously collected in CI centres. Even collection of almanacs

(*Panji*), bus and train timetables, road maps, etc., may prove to be of immense help to the local community.

Public libraries can work as organised resource centres where all the agencies involved in public welfare may be asked to go on supplying regularly and religiously all their update information brochures and publicity materials for proper dissemination of information to the people calling on libraries for aforesaid enquiries.

Trained library staff can extend the professional assistance to community groups in the work of acquisition and cataloguing—classification—indexing of information materials and obviously, prompt dissemination of these information to the intending users. The CI centres can also be profitably utilised for post-literacy drive for the growing number of neo-literates.

Manual of Community Information Service

Once we decide to introduce CIS in our public libraries, we should prepare a manual of CIS incorporating therein a list of all the possible types and varieties of information queries and services that can be offered to users and also a compiled list of available current information booklets that can answer such queries.

This manual can best be compiled based on opinion survey of our target users, group discussions among librarians, joint discussions between library authorities and other government agencies and survey of the publicity and information materials produced by different agencies, like central and different State government ministries, departments, directorates and research bodies. Once such manual is prepared, copies of it can be supplied to different public libraries and librarians themselves will be free to make choice from it of the information services that they would like to offer to their clientele fitting the particular needs of the locality and collect accordingly the supporting information booklets published by different government and research bodies.

Model Town and Rural Library for introducing of CIS

It is high time now for the library directorates of all the States where public library act has already been introduced to implement the CIS scheme, at least to start it on an experimental basis in one model town and one rural library. Taking lessons from their experiences, full-fledged CIS can be introduced in the second phase in all the public libraries of the States. With the beginning of the twentyfirst century we can thus extend our public library services to the grass roots levels.

CLIC—A New Attempt in West Bengal

Incidentally, it may be mentioned that the Department of Mass Education has recently started a project to establish CLICs (Community Library & Information Centres) in Panchayat areas which are not yet covered by sponsored libraries. A report says, till September 2000, 341 CLICs have been established under the supervision of Zila Parishads. But in all respect, these appear to serve only as a miniature model of CIS.

CIS Guarantees Popularity and Wider User Base for Public Libraries

For the sake of stronger democratic foundation of the country, we look forward for early implementation of CIS. Once the neighbouring community starts enjoying the advantage of getting all the necessary information from the nearest library-*cum*-CI Centre, they need not have to bother where to go for what information. Libraries will thus automatically become popular, with wider user base, and people will very often voluntarily step in the library with the prospect of gradually being attracted to the world of knowledge and recreation through book and non-book media. With the successful implementation of CIS, our public libraries will also become, as a popular slogan once coined in Britain, 'a place to go when you don't know where to go'.

8

CIS—The New Horizon of Public Library Services

The oft-quoted abbreviated term CIS stands for Community Information Service, which literally means information service for the (local) community. But the term 'community' may often lead to confusion drawing analogy from the wider term 'anthropology'. It should, therefore, be clarified at the outset that the public library service providers have nothing to do with any particular clan or anthropological group of people. Then 'community' simply means the local or the neighbouring people, irrespective of caste-creed-sex and social or economic status living around any public library. More precisely we should say that this CIS aims particularly at the lower strata of the society—the poor and downtrodden people of the society—who have no access to any other source of information needed for their daily life. Keeping in mind the urgent needs of their daily livelihood, particularly for improving their quality of life, this CIS has been conceived and is now being implemented throughout the world. In view of this interpretation, CIS may be broadly classified as an essential Social Information Service.

The CIS has been explained from different standpoints by various people at different corners. One such explanation comes from a leading librarian of America who has defined it as an "information needed to cope with crises in the lives of individuals and communities". [Donohue Joseph C., '*Community Information Services—A Proposed Definition.*] Donohue has further elaborated this concise definition and said that this information service is of two kinds—first one is 'Survival information', which is related mainly with health, housing, earnings, legal protection, financial aids and opportunities, political rights, etc. The second one is, 'Citizen action information', which is necessary for participation, as an individual or as a member of a bigger group, in the areas of social, political, economic or legal activities. [Allan Bunch, *The Basics of Community Information Work*, London, Library Association Publishing, 1993.] Later, the Library Association of UK has further elaborated the concept of CIS and has explained it as—those which 'assist individuals and groups with daily problem solving and with participation in the democratic process. The services concentrate on the needs of those who do not have ready access to other sources of assistance and on the most important problems that people have to face, problems to do with their homes, their jobs and their rights'. [*Community Information—What Libraries can do*, London, Library Association, 1980.]

Incidentally, we may refer to another explanation, which highlights the philosophical base of Community Information Service; it is essentially 'a logical response to demonstrated need for non-book information about community resources'. [Clara S. Jones, (ed.), *Public Library Information and Referral Service*, Gaylord Professional Publications, 1978.]

As the idea of community information service first cropped up abroad—particularly in UK and America during the post-Second World War era, so also the public library-based community information service has now crossed the century to take a well-developed permanent place in those countries. Centring round the principal location of any public library, many of its branches, even sometimes more than 100 in number, have developed in different places—from where CIS is being provided to its respective local areas. This CIS is, of course, always rendered as a part of their total literary service. By virtue of this service, those libraries are gradually becoming more and more popular and pro-people in nature. As for example, we may cite the names of some leading CIS centres in countries like America, England,

Canada, Australia, etc.: (1) 'North Star Net' (USA): it is a popular community information network available at greater Chicago area. This 24-hour information service is organised by North Suburban Library System and 64 local libraries representing 124 communities. Information on local historical sites with photos-maps-pictures, current engagements-events-meetings, employment news, programmes of local libraries, names and addresses of local health centres, educational institutions, banks and other essential service centres, and notable personalities of the localities, etc., are available on this network. (2) CIS conducted by Independence Township Library and Library of Michigan (USA). (3) CIS by Chenoa, Illinois (USA)—giving information on public utility telephone numbers, meetings and engagements, agricultural cooperatives, sports and games, commerce and business, churches-parks-clubs, entertainments, education, tourism, etc. (4) Memphis Shelby County Public Library and Information Centre (USA)—giving information on various meetings-functions-engagements. (5) Alaska Community Database: C.I. Summaries (USA)—highlights information on local topography, population, tax and levies, weather, history, culture, schools, health, economy, transportation, etc. (6) MARC 21 Concise Format for Community Information—giving references of local leaders and social workers, local municipal and other institutional services, local artists, blood-banks and driving-training schools, special lectures and meetings, etc. (7) Cascadelink, Portland/Vancouver (Canada)—gives all sorts of local information service to the citizen, links with Washington State University Library and other information services through network. (8) Community Information Toronto (Canada)—aims at giving social information service to the local people. (9) Community Information Strategies, Australia (CISA)—this information service centre of South Australia keeps the local people constantly informed of all latest and correct information, so that they can take necessary information-based decisions and take part in social enterprises. (10) Community Information Victoria, Melbourne (Australia)—engaged in giving local people free unbiased personal information service through its fifty information centres. Statewise 'database' or 'Thesaurus' have been compiled and are kept here to help the permanent residents and the visitors. There is also regular in-house training for the information workers. (11) Community Information Service—Hamilton Public Library (Australia) is also very popular, which has a collection of 'online database' of more than 4,500 records. It specialises in non-profit information service on 'Health' rendered by government and NGO sources. (12) Devon Library and Information Service (UK)—gives information service on 'child care', 'social health', 'voluntary service'—which in short may be termed as 'something for everyone' or 'information on anything and everything'. (13) Craigmillar Community Information Service (CCIS), Edinburgh (UK)—gives information service to the local people, which includes information on local organisations, adult education centres, festivals, housing projects, technical education facilities, etc. (14) Last, but not the least, is the information service provided by the New York Public Library—which includes detailed information or emergency information about the local community or the people in the adjoining areas through its widespread network branches. The people of Manhattan-Bronx-Statin Island can avail of the prompt information provided by a few hundreds of the local not-for-profit organisations through its Directory of Community Services in English and Spanish language. These are all, of course, online database information instantly provided through computers. But it should be particularly mentioned that in all branches of New York Public Library a special 'Community Information Service Collection', consisting of handbooks, guides, pamphlets and brochures, is also maintained.

In our country, when we are thinking, and planning as well, of introducing library-based CIS, we must then keep in mind this printed 'CIS collection' of New York Public Library. Information is now a commodity and that, too, is costly. Moreover, information technology is also not very popularly available in our widespread rural-based society. Above all, the 'have-nots' or the poor-neglected-exploited people for whom we are planning to provide CIS, do not have facilities, technical expertise or financial capabilities to avail of the computer or internet services. We, therefore, need to concentrate on collection of printed information booklets or handbooks. In view of our present socio-economic condition, this would be our correct step.

We must further clarify our ideas before we discuss the necessary preparatory steps that we should now undertake. We need to clarify how our proposed CIS is related to the public libraries or, in other words, why we are thinking to render the CIS through the public library system. Firstly, we need to expand the area of public library service. From our experience, we have noticed that the public libraries which are engaged only in the traditional service of lending books can no more attract readers in big way. Library service confined only within lending of books is no more considered as adequate to serve the needs of the day. It is high time to appreciate that we cannot continue 'marketing only with limited old stock'. We need new input, new ideas, new steps. Keeping in view the present day needs of the people, the CIS has, therefore, been introduced. As it is already stated, CIS has been fairly introduced in public libraries of Western countries and that, too, has gradually improved on public demand. Now it is equally necessary to introduce CIS in our public libraries. Once we can do it, the gradually declining readership will improve, the libraries will also become more popular and people-oriented. Secondly, public libraries can be the fittest social organisations through which information service can be best rendered in most effective and easiest way. Public libraries are already having necessary infrastructure and professionally trained employees who are in a better position to classify and catalogue the non-book materials and information collection and can also do the necessary job of their indexing, shelving, retrieval and prompt supply to the users. Hence, public libraries can be comparatively better choice than other types of available information centres for rendering CIS. Thirdly, once we can merge the Community Information Centres with the rural and urban primary-level public libraries, the number of users will be considerably increased and consequently, our national democratic base will be further strengthened. Fourthly, the unnecessary tendency to channelise community information service through multifarious organisations can be checked.

Incidentally, it may be mentioned that recently various types of 'information kiosks' or information marketing centres are being developed in parallel with the CIS. Like other countries, we too are now having some such kiosks. These are independent of library system, mostly connected with business and commercial marketing or with government publicity-mechanism. These are in no way connected with libraries. To cite an example, the Government of West Bengal, in collaboration with Webel and BSNL, has planned to set up information kiosk in every district with the object of disseminating government rules and regulations and information about various development projects to the common people who generally have no access to internet. Reliance Infocom Co. also plans to set up e-governance projects in six States like Madhya Pradesh, Tamil Nadu and some northern States whereby land revenue and other taxation departments of the respective States will be connected from the headquarters to lowest units. They are also setting up information kiosks from cities to villages. Other multinational companies like TCS, IBM, Microsoft, etc., are also moving in the same line. Through e-choupal of ITC company efforts are also being made for providing information or for marketing products to the farmers up to the village level. In Kerala, the public sector company Keltron is also engaged in setting up Information Kiosk to bridge the gap between the rich and the poor prevailing in the electronic age. But we must always keep in mind the fundamental difference between all these devices and the CIS. The CIS is essentially a modern important part of the comprehensive library service.

In Western countries, along with the introduction of outreach programme, the leading social scientists and the library experts simultaneously conceived jointly the community information service. As a result of which there came an opportunity to improve the quality of life of the common people. Utterly disappointed poor people gradually became interested to avail of this information service. They learnt to solve themselves many of their problems. As self-learning is possible through studies in libraries, these CIS centres too, offer self-help scope. Hence, libraries and information centres are justifiably called "poor man's university". [Allan Bunch, *Community Information Services*, London: Clive Bingley, 1982.]

Thus our experiences show that by introducing CIS in public libraries, lower middle class people are mostly benefited. Even the illiterate people are used to visit those libraries in search of information and gradually they feel interested to read books and newspapers after being trained in the adult-education centres of those libraries. Thus increases the number of library-users who can derive pleasure through reading on their own initiative. In fine, as CIS can satisfy the needs of daily-life in many ways, so also it can play a major role in improving the standard of life of the poor backward people of the society. The foundation of democracy can also be strengthened in this way. Hence, CIS is now a challenge for the library-lovers. With the aid of CIS, a public library can become a place which can be termed as—'A place to go when you don't know where to go'—if we don't know where to go (to satisfy our query), let us go to the library—once such popular slogan of Britain will eventually be very familiar to all. Information seeking people will then very easily and unhesitantly enter a library—neighbours won't mind for that as they could cast aspersion if he enters a divorce-office or credit society office to seek relevant information. On the backdrop of this experience and objective, community information service will develop in our country in near future. Public libraries and the Community Information Centres can also be effectively utilised for implementing post-literacy programmes for the growing neo-literates. [As per Census 2001, literacy rate has grown up by 13.17% during the last ten years and thus reached 65.38% in 2001. As such, in every 100 persons, 35 persons are still illiterate. We shall have to go a long way in the literacy and post-literacy campaign.]

While introducing CIS, emphasis has always been given to local issues. In the third edition of UNESCO Public Library Manifesto 1994, it is stated that public libraries must render necessary information service on 'local enterprise, local organisations and local issues' and must satisfy the information needs of all age-groups. The manifesto has clearly stated that public libraries will act as 'gateway to local information', where the users can avail of all the sources of knowledge and information whose 'high quality and relevance to local needs and conditions are fundamental'. Based on this objective, necessary emphasis has been given to compilation of local history in the CIS centres abroad. Basically, it is needed that various historical elements in respect of local history-tradition-education-culture or architecture must be carefully compiled in the public library based CIS centres. As these local-histories will satisfy the queries of the local people, similarly, based on these local histories, history researcher may one day compile a new democratic foundation of a bigger comprehensive national history. As a garland is made by stitching together many flowers taking one by one, similarly the garland of national history can be compiled with flower-like elements of various local histories taking one by one.

Incidentally, in case of our own country we may think of making some additional collection. As for example, if in any remote rural library and information centre, we can collect, along with the local history, also a few State Level or national level information booklets like that on tourism, higher education and professional training, sports or various State and Central government grants in different fields, then the aspiring local youths will be much benefited.

In fact, the main basis of community information service is the 'right to information'. The more we can make it wider and universal, the more will be the foundation of democracy stronger.

In this context, we may take note of the variety and importance of the demand for community information in our country. As for example, there is need or demand for information on municipal or Panchayat rules and regulations, and the facilities available therefrom, government grants for various social development projects, e.g., Swarnajayanti self-employment project, total rural income planning, Indira housing plan, Antyodya and Annapurana Yojana, Employment-guarantee project, Prime Minister's Rural Welfare Project etc., venues and time-schedule of adult education, centres for obtaining unemployment aid or widow pension scope for specialised treatment (like that of Aids or Leprosy), family planning, agriculture or house loan, cooperative training, prices and addresses of local dealers of weaver's thread – fertiliser – seeds – detergents – irrigation equipments – oil – pump – tractor – fishing equipments etc., place and time schedule for local entertainment – sports and games – religious talks and mythological story-telling, folksong contests, etc. For instant answers to queries on such issues, planned collection of information booklets at the information centres is essential. Even almanacs or bus-train time tables should also be collected and kept ready at the information centres.

Before we set up Community Information Service Centres based on the aforesaid information queries in our State, we must conduct one users' survey. It was revealed in a district-wise preliminary survey in West Bengal during the first-half of the last nineties that the average number of readers of government and government-aided libraries was only 1 per cent of the population of the neighbouring areas, whereas this number was 15 per cent to 25 per cent in foreign countries, even it was 33 per cent in some countries. In view of this miserable preliminary statistics, it appears that we need immediately more wider survey. We must know exactly what percentage of the total population of the State are members or users of the government and government-aided libraries. From the voters list for Municipality, Panchayat and Assembly elections and the Census Report (of 2011), we can find out the total number of literate person in each district and the total number of members of the libraries of the State. From these two figures, we can find out the desired percentage figure. This figure can be compared with the total amount spent annually for the library services in the State. We must also think seriously why the major portion of our population are detached from the public libraries and what is the justifiability of spending growing amount of money for such a limited number of readers. We hope, out of this thinking we will ultimately be convinced of the urgent need to introduce community information service.

Now let us concentrate on some of the primary steps that we need to take for introducing this public library-based community information service. Firstly, conducting one local survey, i.e., analysing the nature of the neighbouring population around the proposed library—their main occupation—how many people are agriculturist/industrial worker/middle class employee/businessman—economic condition—schools-colleges: number of male-female students—standard of education—percentage of literacy, etc. Secondly, survey of expected queries relating to necessity of life and occupation and areawise survey of types of information—queries that may emanate from the local community. A manual may be compiled on the basis of these surveys—which will contain a full list of community information service that can be rendered. Thirdly, to find out, in support of the information services, what are the printed or unprinted books or documents, i.e., books, magazines, reference books, daily newspapers and local papers, as well as what are the official and unofficial publications, i.e., publicity materials/departmental brochures/information booklets/trade literature, etc., are available for purchase or on gift or exchange. A second manual should also be compiled based on the aforesaid findings. Of course, both these manuals should be regularly updated. Based on the local users' survey, as stated before, and the aforesaid two manuals, village/town or region based librarians can set up their targets of CIS as may be suitable for their respective area libraries and would accordingly try to collect the necessary information booklets for their respective libraries. In all the States, like West Bengal and others, where the Public Library Act is in vogue, Community Information Service can thus be introduced through an integrated public library system.

Incidentally, it should be mentioned that the aforesaid two manuals should be compiled by following certain norms and procedures. As for instance, survey of opinions of the expected users, seminars of librarians at different levels, joint meetings of the library authority and the government officials, survey of the huge number of publicity and information booklet published on behalf of the State/Central Ministry/Department/Directorate and the various research organisations, etc., can be utilised for making the proposed manuals most representative in nature and content. After compiling these manuals, these copies can be sent to various libraries. Then the respective librarians themselves can determine which of the CI services may be relevant for their respective areas and accordingly they would try to collect regularly and sincerely the relevant helpful information booklets as are mentioned in the manuals.

To make this proposed scheme most effective, a few 'model' libraries in the States may be chosen for introducing CIS, with coordinating help and support of the Raja Rammohun Roy Library Foundation. Based on the experience of success or failure or impediments in the initial venture, a full-fledged operational scheme can be worked out to introduce CIS throughout the States.

CIS is indeed a challenge in the new era with new hopes and it will eventually prove that the book-service and the information service can be complementary to each other in the public library-based CIS centres.

9

CIS—A New Dimension of Public Library Service

Readership Survey reveals Poor Public Interest in Libraries

One of the yardsticks for measuring the popularity of a public library may be its membership strength. But merely the membership figure does not reveal the whole picture. It is rather more relevant to know how many people of its neighbouring area are using the library, and to find out such data it is essential to conduct readership or users' survey. As such, surveys are often conducted to feel the pulse of the public library activities. Readership surveys, as conducted particularly in the UK, USA or other Western countries, have revealed that the public libraries generally serve only 25 per cent to 33 per cent of the total population. Bernard Berelson in his famous study 'The library's public' (1949) identified that public libraries served only 15 per cent to 25 per cent of the population in the UK. The later surveys in the UK revealed that this coverage hardly went up to 33 per cent of the population. [Allan Bunch, 'Community Information Services'. London: Clive Bingley, 1982.] In our country, of course, there has not been any such significant methodical survey of public library users. But on notional basis, it can be said that our readership coverage is in no way better, if not worse, in view of higher percentage of illiteracy in our country. One very dismal picture has been revealed in a recent status report prepared by the Directorate of Library Services, West Bengal. The report has given district-wise number of government and sponsored libraries (1991-92) in West Bengal, along with their total membership (adult and children) figure, against the population figure (1991 Census) of each district. On an analysis of the report it is found that the total membership of all government and sponsored libraries of the State hardly covers one per cent (1%) of the total population of the State. [Dr. S.R. Ranganathan Birth Centenary Workshop on the Public Library System in West Bengal, 11th-13th September, 1992, Salt Lake, Calcutta: Working Papers.]

Besides these membership percentages, the other feature of the readership base, as revealed by various surveys, is that the majority of the readers of public libraries represent by and large the middle class of the society. The upper class people generally think it below their status and prestige to come to the public library to avail of its services, while the lower socio-economic group of people have no interest, nor any leisure-time or literary capability for using public library services. In such a situation, the majority of the population are kept out of the purview of the services and benefits of public libraries, despite the fact that these libraries are funded from public exchequer.

Urge for Expansion of Users' Base

This appeared to be a sheer wastage of public money and public energy as well. The worldwide library profession as a whole became much concerned about such a situation and by the sixties to seventies of the last century, social leaders started thinking of a way out of effective utilisation of public library services. The obvious means was to expand the users' base, which was in turn dependent on the library leaders' capability in creating public interest in library services. Concerted attempts were, therefore, made to achieve this goal. Among many other measures, Community Information Service (CIS) was one major outcome of these attempts during the last few decades, which provided an opportunity to expand the users' base, particularly to reach the poor who comprise the majority section of the society.

Emerging New Concept of Library and Librarianship

Thus the library organisers became primarily involved in creating public interest and attracting them towards libraries. Consequently, the concept of library services has also undergone a sea change during the last few decades, both in Western countries as well as in Indian context.

The traditional idea of library as a storehouse of knowledge confined within the pages of printed books only is rather obsolete now-a-days, and obviously the librarian is also no more regarded as a mere keeper or custodian of books. Bidding farewell to the traditional custodian mentality, the librarian has to assume now-a-days the role of a social leader of the people around his neighbouring society with the key task of satisfying, their needs and demands for information—may be for educational, cultural or leisure purposes. To achieve this social task the librarian has to collect, along with books, various other non-book materials (NBM) which have proved to be essential tools for achieving his goal. Aided with these NBM tools the librarian can invite and attract the people to call on the library and then retrieve and present the desired information to his invitee clientele, many of whom are obviously illiterate, and thereby giving them utmost satisfaction with a touch of pleasant surprise indeed.

New Dimension of Public Library Service—CIS

Thus in a changing scenario, the public library is committed to satisfy the users' needs and demands for various information. The public library is, therefore, being equipped accordingly and is now-a-days very often termed as a 'library resource centre' (LRC). Its services may be broadly classified into two main heads, one is the traditional book service, and the other is the newly developed non-book service. Among the non-book services are generally included the Outreach Programme (as is previously termed the Extension Programme), Audio-visual service and Information service. This information service is further specified as the Information & Referral Service (I & RS), which, in other words, is very often referred to as the Community Information Service (CIS). An expert opinion has explained the CIS as "a logical response to demonstrate need for non-book information about community resources" [Clara S. Jones (ed.), 'Public Library Information & Referral Service', Gaylord Professional Publications, 1978.] In view of the increasing needs and demands for information by the downtrodden people of the society and with the emergence of new concept of public library services, CIS is now gaining more and more popularity throughout the world and, obviously, India cannot remain away from this changing scenario. In fact, this has, of late, emerged as a challenge to us. Successful implementation of CIS through our public libraries would indeed help us to strengthen the democratic foundation of our country.

Of course, it should always be kept in mind that this new information service is in no way going to replace the traditional book service, rather it has developed as complementary to the early book service.

Our National Policy also aims at Developing CIS

The Committee set up by the Government of India under the Chairmanship of Prof. D.P. Chattopadhyay for formulating a National Policy on Library & Information System in India submitted its report in May 1986. In its recommendations about our Public Library System, the Committee emphasised on the need to introduce community libraries in rural areas. It states: 'The most important task before the Government is to establish, maintain and strengthen the free public libraries in the country and enable them to work as a system. The main thrust in this area should go to the rural public library. A village or a village cluster with an adequate population should have a community library which will also serve as an information centre. Resources of different agencies engaged in the work of public health, adult education, local self-government and such others may be pooled to build up this composite centre'.

UNESCO Recommendations for Public Libraries

The UNESCO Public Library Manifesto 1972/1994 may also be referred to in this context as a most valuable relevant document which recommends collection of NBM or AVM (audio-visual materials) along with books, in public libraries for developing education, culture and information services. 'The Manifesto proclaims UNESCO's belief in the public library as a living force for education, culture and information.'

What is meant by Community Information?

While appreciating the need to develop CIS through our public libraries, we must clarify what is meant by Community Information. As the Library Association of UK has a long tradition of introducing and developing CIS, we may take special note of their concept of community information. They have explained CIS as 'a positive decision to concentrate or enabling people, particularly those in lower socio-economic groups, to act either individually or collectively on their problems in the fields of housing, employment, family and personal matters, consumer affairs, household finance, education, welfare rights and civil rights'. For further clarification, Library Association has defined CIS as 'services which assist individuals and groups with daily problem-solving and with participation in the democratic process. The services concentrate on the needs of those who do not have ready access to other sources of assistance and on the most important problems that people have to face, problems to do with their homes, their jobs and their rights'. [*Community Information: What Libraries can do—A Consultative Document.*— London: Library Association, 1980]

Poor Man's University

In Western countries, during the early days of developing outreach programmes in public libraries, community information was also seen as a means whereby the "quality of life" could be raised. It should allow people to extend themselves, take initiatives, broaden their sphere of competence, be enterprising. This self-help function is very much aligned with the public library ethos of individualised learning. There was a time in the early days of the movement when the public library was referred to as the "poor man's university". [Allan Bunch, *ibid.*]

In short, community information is provided to help people 'with daily problem solving or in raising the quality of their lives', and it serves 'those who belong to the lower socio-economic groups or are disadvantaged'.

Types of Community Information and their Helpful Use

As social being, people have various types of information-queries in relation to their problems and needs of day-to-day life. It is the duty of the public librarian to meticulously collect and supply the necessary information booklets to satisfy such queries to their clientele as and when they call on him for the purpose. CI may cover a very wide field of our day-to-day needs, e.g., information on housing and other cooperative/bank loan systems, government-loans for various social projects, self-employment schemes, employment opportunities, location and facilities of rural/agricultural banks, prices and availability of various agricultural inputs (like seed, fertilizer, insecticide, oil and pump set, tractor, etc.), and also fishery and cottage or small-scale industry inputs, seed/soil testing centres, local markets for their products, scope for primary/secondary/vocational education and training for their young wards, adult education provisions, hospital/medicare services, Panchayat and cooperative society rules, and so on. Current supporting booklets on such varied information should be judiciously collected. Even collection of almanacs (*Panji*), bus and train time-tables, road maps, etc., may prove to be of immense help to the local community.

Public libraries can work as organised resource centres where all the agencies involved in public welfare may be asked to go on supplying regularly and religiously all their up-to-date information brochures and publicity materials for proper dissemination of information to the people calling on the libraries for aforesaid enquiries.

Trained library staff can extend the professional assistance to community groups in the work of acquisition of materials, cataloguing-classification-indexing of information materials and, obviously, prompt dissemination of those information to their users as and when asked for.

Manual of Community Information Service

Once we decide to introduce CIS in our public libraries, we should prepare a manual of CIS incorporating therein a list of all the possible types and varieties of information queries and services that can be offered to users and also a compiled list of available current information booklets that can answer such queries. The manual can best be compiled based on opinion survey of our target users, group discussion among librarians, joint discussions between authorities of public libraries and other government agencies and a survey of the publicity and information materials produced by different agencies, say, in our State, by different departments and directorates of the Government of West Bengal. Once such a manual is prepared, copies of it can be supplied to different public libraries and librarians themselves will be free to make choice from it of the information services that they would like to offer to their clientele befitting the particular needs of the locality and collect accordingly the supporting information booklets published by different government departments.

Model Town and Rural Library may be selected to Introduce CIS

It is high time now for the library directorates of all the States where Public Library Act has already been introduced to implement CIS scheme, at least to start it on an experimental basis. At the beginning, a few Town and Rural Libraries may be selected for the purpose. Taking lessons from the experience of such introductory CIS and critically reviewing the areas of their success or difficulties, full-fledged CIS can be introduced in the second phase in all the public libraries of the States.

Training of Library Personnel is Essential for the Purpose

Library professionals must be specially trained for proper handling and processing of NBM, so that they can effectively respond to hundreds of information-queries. But besides this professional expertise, all that is needed most is an appreciative attitude towards CIS.

Quality of Service Must Also Improve

But the users cannot be satisfied if the quality of service is not improved. The information that is provided must be accurate, detailed and up-to-date and at the same time, the Reference Librarian must be prompt and alert, with an obvious helpful and sympathetic attitude towards his clientele. Adequate arrangements must also be made to ensure that all sorts of information may be available under one roof. Let us hope that with the cooperation of all agencies and library professionals, we would soon be able to reach such an ideal situation, when people will feel free to come to CI centres and neighbours will not have unnecessary speculations as to why he is going to CI centre (as very often happens when one goes to divorce-consultants or loan-centres).

Popularity and Wider User Base

Once the neighbouring community starts enjoying the advantage of getting all the necessary information from the nearest library, they need not have to bother where to go for what information. Libraries will thus automatically become popular, with wider user base, and people will very often voluntarily step in the library with the prospect of gradually being attracted to the world of knowledge and recreation through book and non-book media. With the successful implementation of CIS, our public libraries will also become, as a popular slogan once coined in Britain, 'A place to go when you don't know where to go'.

10

Reversing the Digital Divide: Reaching out to the Information Have-nots

The term 'Information Have-nots' indeed is having a wider connotation in respect of our society. It is our painful experience to find economic disparity all around us in our country today. In fact, gross inequity is the main characteristic of Indian society today. There are two distinctive groups of "haves" and "havenots" in our society. Obviously, the vast majority—about 85 per cent of our population—represents the "have-nots" and this stands in respect of their worldly possessions, their social status and financial position of their families. But the most interesting fact is this that the "economic have-nots" status also makes them—in most cases—"information have-nots". When I say that mostly the poor downtrodden people suffer from lack of information, I mean that those people do not have any access to information necessary for the development of quality of life. In other words, an innumerable number of poor people, clustered around some pockets of both the urban and rural areas, who may be unlettered but not illiterate, severely lack many of their daily problem-solving information. Precisely, we may call this type of information as the 'community information', and the people who are keen to develop public library services through their outreach programmes in most parts of the world are now providing this much needed Community Information Service.

Before we talk further about CIS, we may see why and how the Digital Divide in our society has occurred.

There is a sharp divide between two groups of citizens—one is "online citizens", and the other who have no access to internet services may be called "non-internet citizens". The fact remains that this second group of people constitutes the vast majority of our population who are generally poor and disadvantaged. This disparity has created the digital divide.

One approach to Reversing the Digital Divide and thus to bridge the digital gap between the two groups of citizens may be (i) to provide free access to the internet at every public library, and the other may be (ii) to provide community information service to the downtrodden people through various outreach programmes of the public libraries. In view of huge dearth of necessary infrastructure and widening disparity in literacy among the people in our country—both the online database and printed information booklets may be provided through our public libraries, as is done in New York State Public Library. Such a pragmatic coexistence of both may be the right approach at the moment. Otherwise only internet approach may be utopian in our present day society.

One of the distinguished professional librarians of America, Joseph C. Donohue has defined Community Information Service as the "Information needed to cope with crises in the lives of individuals and communities". There are two types of information—one is 'Survival information', which is related mainly with problems of Health, Housing, Earnings, Legal Safety, Financial aids and opportunities, Political rights, etc. The other type of information is 'Citizen Action Information', which is needed for participation in socio-political activities. The Library Association of UK has further elaborated the community information as "those which assist individuals and groups with daily problem-solving and with participation in the democratic process. The CIS concentrate on the needs of those who do not have ready access to other sources of assistance and on the most important problems that people have to face, problems to do with their homes, their jobs and their rights".

All these types of Community Information can be promptly provided by Public Libraries through their own 'online database'.

This type of CIS is of late very popular in most of the developed countries like US, Canada, UK, Australia and others and the other developing countries including India are also devoting their time and energy to develop this 'online database' community information service to their urban and rural clients. But here comes the question of digital divide and the library service captains are now busy to find out means of reversing the digital divide and to reach the Information Have-nots as much as possible. As referred to before, the New York State Public Library, besides their online database has also developed in all their branches a special 'Community Information Service Collection' which consists of 'handbooks, guides, pamphlets and brochures'. This collection has its special attraction for 'Information Have-nots'. It can be a model to follow elsewhere.

There are information gaps even in case of elite society. We may concentrate on providing them more of the Information & Communication Technologies (ICTs) and infrastructure facilities, and as such we can fill up the loopholes and improve the existing position, and may feel proud to have achieved international standard at least in our technical libraries and research centres. There are suggestions for its improvement. We may like to fully upgrade hardware and software and make arrangements to ensure that the latest programmes are available to service use. Even we may like to abolish charges for internet access in public libraries. Steps may be taken to build the basic infrastructures like electricity, telephone and internet connectivity in the rural areas. But still that will not help reversing the digital divide. We are concerned about growing gap between information-rich and information-poor. We may have to go further to make internet services more accessible and acceptable to the common people who are still bracketed as information have-nots.

If we can provide wide-network services throughout our rural areas and think of achieving the task of reversing the digital divide, we may be mistaken. The infrastructure facilities and information and communication technologies (ICTs) alone cannot solve the problem of digital divide, until and unless we can change the mind-set and develop the proper mental aptitude and literary capabilities at the receiving end where millions of people are living below poverty line—undernourished and half-fed, deprived of primary education, health services, employment and other civic facilities. Hence the task is two-fold which must be undertaken hand-in-hand together to achieve our target of reversing digital divide.

Before I conclude, I submit that meanwhile, other steps may also be taken and new areas of outreach programmes may be explored to improve the public library services which may be the best channel for reversing digital divide.

11

Industrial Library Perspectives

With the growth and modernisation of industries, industrial libraries are coming up steadily. It is true for all the places, and obviously, West Bengal is no exception. But to be more precise, it is only with the end of the Second World War that the industrial libraries have started developing in and around Calcutta. And from the sixties onwards, when there has been an explosion of information and data, these have started gaining importance. Industrial libraries in the State are now holding a significant place in the ever-expanding field of library services, and naturally, these are now attracting more and more talents.

In most of the cases, the overseas companies operating in our areas first started taking initiative in setting up library and information centres in their own industries. Gradually the Indian industrialists, and even some of our public sector authorities, who are keen on introducing modern methods and ideas, joined hands with the multinational companies and started appreciating the significant role that these industrial libraries can play. Some of the engineering and the chemical industries in the eastern sector first established such libraries, and gradually other types of industries, both in private and public sectors, opted for the same.

Industrial libraries have their own specialities, not much in common with the general characteristics of the public library system. They are more oriented towards management of data and information than towards the acquisition and circulation of traditional books. Handling of micro thoughts is more prevalent in their approach, and documentation services are more needed by their clientele. Here updated reference books both technical and commercial are more in demand than traditional text books, and technical articles in current periodicals, mostly of foreign origin, are much needed to keep its users apprised of the latest technological developments taking place in the advanced countries. In the case of multinational companies, their technical libraries need to handle a huge number of technical correspondence, mostly with their overseas counterparts or technical collaborators. Technology transfer is now the cry of the day, and a well-equipped industrial library and information centre has a big role to play for its successful implementation.

Besides the aforesaid library materials, another type of important literature very often bother the industrial librarian. A huge number of varied trade literature, mostly on new products or raw materials, or machinery and equipment, are continuously damped on the librarian's desk. These are mostly collected by the company's technical people during their visits to international trade fairs or the suppliers' overseas plants. Such visits are very frequent and result-oriented in case of progressive and expanding companies and as such, it is imperative on the part of the company's information centre to preserve these manufactures' trade literature and to systematically arrange them for ready reference. It is obviously not an easy task, and is being done with care and intelligence devising some suitable techniques, like compiling manufacturers' index or product index, with cross reference, and so on, for quick retrieval of necessary information. In fact, industrial librarian thus takes care to build up his data bank very much needed by his clientele. The trade literature as referred to here has very often proved to be an essential tool at the time of selection and acquisition of new machineries and equipment or for establishing new raw materials or products.

Sometimes industrial librarians are also required to handle numerous standard specifications or important designs and drawings, maps, etc. Incidentally, it should be mentioned that such library centres must strictly avoid staff recreational books and journals, as they are supposed to lead to diversion from the original goal of the information centres.

As already emphasised, documentation, including reprographic services, is an essential part of the valuable services rendered by an industrial library. Computers have now added a new dimension to its area of activities. Many industries prefer to process their Management Information Services (MIS) through their library and information centres.

Still the question arises in some quarters whether it is worth investing money for an industrial library. Whether any quick return from a library is possible? Does its cost-benefit analysis prove encouraging? Cost can no doubt be easily computed, but how far it is feasible to assess its direct or indirect benefits? Perhaps all these questions arise when there is lack of real appreciation of an industrial library in its true perspective. After all, like R&D, it is also a long range programme which may reap its harvest only at the opportune moment. We must have patience and bend of mind to allow time to appreciate its real contributions. For running a library in an industry, it doesn't matter how big is the company, or how much is its turnover and profitability, or how big is the number of its employees; the most important factor that matters is the outlook of the management; the more progressive is their outlook, the more success can be achieved through developing a library and information centre within the industry itself.

Let us take an example. There are instances where by virtue of merit and relevance one or two of the many technical abstracts released by the technical library on routine basis happen to catch the notice of the top-boss of the company, and then the ball is set in motion and based on the information provided in the abstract, a series of subsequent chain follow-up takes place, which ultimately lead to successful development and marketing of a new product of the company.

This is only a stray instance where industrial library can offer direct benefit. In fact, there are certain specified phases of industrial development where such libraries may prove more beneficial, e.g., when the industry undertakes some expansion and modernisation programmes, or when it takes up a forward looking manpower planning through regular management development and training programmes, or when it is involved in vigorous Research & Development programmes, services of in-plant library and information centres appear to be essential. More and more data and information must be constantly fed in for successful implementation of the aforesaid programmes, and the services of an well-equipped technical library must prove to be of tremendous help in such a situation.

Such a technical library has its own merits and limitations; it has its own importance and characteristics; and all these must always be kept in mind while evaluating the industrial library perspectives. An essential criterion of such libraries is that they must render very prompt reference service; nothing is supposed to be kept pending there. So it requires more alert library staff. Apart from the professional knowledge and expertise, the librarian must have also adequate acquaintance with the process and technology of the industry he is serving. The industrial librarian and information officer can develop such an acquaintance only through personal study and initiative, provided of course, he has that educational background and intelligence, along with a keen desire and devotion to his profession. The other characteristic of such libraries is that they have limited, and very often, fixed clientele, within the industry, who are more interested in getting direct and readymade information and service, than in going for and searching through library cards and records themselves. Hence, processing of library materials are needed here more by the library staff themselves to render quick service to the users. Another interesting feature of such industrial libraries is that, many of their services are more or less routed in accordance with the organisational hierarchy. As for example, if we look at their circulation lists, which are prepared to facilitate the in-company circulation of journals or various technical extracts, it may be noticed that the literatures are very often routed on priority basis to many a person where there is least chance of being utilised, still the practice is maintained to satisfy the ego of those status conscious officials placed higher up in the organisational structure. However, this is the fact of life, and perhaps, cannot be avoided. But still, all is not wasted. There are at least certain points on the circulation route where the literature is best utilised, and there lies the satisfaction of the librarian.

In fact, it is an area of dealing with the readers' psychology, where the industrial librarian must have some insight. But there are still more things which he is expected to know. A technical librarian and information scientist must know about various facets of documentation, besides being well versed with the techniques of routine processing of library materials; he should also know about reprography, and at the same time, he must get himself acquainted with the computers and their applications in information handling; he should also have some aptitude for technical editing; in fine, he must know his 'industry' and his 'profession' as well. Still, he is not a superman. All that is wanted of him is a keen professional approach, with a broad realistic understanding of the information need of the industry he is serving. All these can be cultivated through a sound professional training, supported by a thorough exposure to industry.

This type of multi-faceted industrial librarianship has of course no proportionate reflection in many of our University curriculum. Our standard syllabus has its own limitations, resulting mainly from the time-constraints which our courses must suffer from. After all, the Universities are committed to train librarians for the whole society catering to the needs of all types of libraries, like academic libraries from school to university level, or public libraries from State to village level, or research libraries and other special or specialised libraries. A time-bound common syllabus cannot, therefore, do justice to all such diversified specialisation. To develop industrial librarianship at the post-graduate teaching level, it can at best introduce some special paper in the syllabus or arrange a couple of months' exposure to industry after the academic session is over. As in the case of engineering and technology, so also in the field of industrial librarianship perhaps a time has come when we should think in terms of developing a close liaison between the academics and the industrialists so that we can produce and feed the right type of professionals for the growing needs of industrial libraries of our country.

Before we conclude, it must of course be admitted that industrial libraries in our country are still lagging behind in comparison to their counterparts in the Western countries. This is as much because of the majority of our industry stalwarts (both in public and private sector) lack of consciousness about the significant role that these libraries can play towards the development of industries, so much also due to lack of adequate number of trained personnel in the profession. The latter shortcoming obviously has developed from the first, and a desired improvement in the situation can only be achieved through a joint effort of the industry and the profession.

12

New Horizon of Book Preservation

Trees are being destroyed in large scale—we are all concerned in this matter on very justified reason. But are we aware of the fact that books are also being destroyed in large scale? We are concerned about 'dying forests', but not so conscious about the fearful aspects of 'dying books'. The pages full of words, 'tied up with the chain of black types', within the two covers are gradually becoming brittle and discoloured—millions of books are thus on the brink of death. Consequently, our cultural heritage as a whole is at stake.

So long we have been alarmed about the attacks of worms and insects. Particularly in tropical countries like ours, attacks of worms and insects are in no way can be neglected. There is no limit of how many millions of books, manuscripts and documents, have been destroyed by attacks of insects and fungus. If the immortal manuscript of Vaishnab literary poem like *Shrikrishnakirtan* would have been kept neglected for some time more at the upper floor of a cowshed in a remote village of Bankura district (West Bengal), there was every possibility that one such immensely valuable treasure of Bengali literature could have been lost forever. That is why all our research and efforts for preservation of books were so long mainly concentrated against the attacks of worms, insects and fungus.

There were other dangers too at the beginning of civilisation. In early times natural calamities like fire, flood, etc., had caused many damages to the books. Besides there were also attacks from outside enemies. After Egypt was defeated by attack of Khalifa

Omar, invaluable books of the famous library of Alexandria, one of the best seat of knowledge of the ancient civilisation, were burnt out one by one selectively. It was so stated that the fire of burning of those books kept the public toilets of the city warm for six months. The Norwaygian witty writer Nilskjaer jokingly said that the Arabian officer appointed by the Khalifa to select books for firing made two stamps. He examined the books one by one to see whether the books were anti-Islam. If one is "anti", he used to put on it the stamp of "not following the *Koran*, hence burn it". If the book is not "anti", he used to put on it the other stamp of "following the *Koran*, hence superfluous—so burn it". Hence, none of the books escaped.

That age is now over. Gradually another bigger enemy of books has come to limelight. That is, 'excess acidity' created over the books' paper-surface surrounding environment is mainly responsible for it. Due to air-pollution various types of acid are being accumulated over the paper. As for example, sulphur dioxide (SO_2) present in air reacts with water vapour, in presence of iron and copper particles as catalytic agent, creating sulphuric acid which is being deposited on paper and in turn that breaks the structure of the cellulose fibres—the basic constituent of paper. Consequently, papers are gradually becoming brittle. For this and other reasons papers are becoming brittle and discoloured—like yellowish or darkly reddish. Books are, therefore, becoming unfit for use.

Consciousness about this enemy of books is more prevalent in West than that in East. Perhaps it is first from America that maximum noise was raised about it. Subsequently, this awareness reached other Western countries and then even the Eastern countries. As per the Western specialists, acidic paper is the biggest enemy of books, they opine—'prime culprit: acidic paper'. With this firm belief, they started worldwide campaign to save the books—the symbol and carrier of national heritage and culture—and devised many new methods to save books from decay. Thus opened the new horizon of book preservation.

The main characteristic of this campaign for book

preservation is: firstly, in view of vastness of the damages caused, mass scale preservation methods should also be initiated; secondly, all the restored rare books and documents should again be made freely available to the users and researchers and moreover those should be transferred in new format and medium to make them usable for long for the new generation. Specialists call it a method of 'reformatting', i.e., preserving in new format. For clarification, we should call the process as, firstly, mass deacidification; and secondly, transferring the paper-books to films. The other characteristic of this 'reformatting' process is appreciable as 'reduction' in size, which is scientifically called transferring to 'microform'.

There are various types of 'microform', *viz.*, 'microfilm', 'microfisch', 'microcard', 'aperture card', 'comfisch', etc. Among the various forms of mass reformatting, the mostly used worldwide recognised process is 'micro-filming'. After reducing the full page of a book to 35 mm or 16 mm microfilm, that cannot be read of course by naked eye. For reading it, a special machine like 'microfilm reader' is necessary, when the small sized microfilm reel is put in it, the reduced pages appear one by one on its screen in its previous larger size so that those can be read easily.

With the help of other part of the machine—'the microfilm printer', the print of any full size page, as necessary, can be taken immediately.

This reformatting has indeed opened a new horizon in the field of book preservation. By this process the original book or document can undergo deacidification and then can be reinforced by necessary lamination and be kept separately as a specially restored master copy. And for regular use, readers and researchers may be supplied with the microfilm copy as a service copy. As such, there will be no chance for the book or the document to be destroyed and readers and researchers will not be deprived of the opportunity to use them for the next hundred years or more. The first newspaper of India—*Hicky's Bengal Gazette* (1780) is undoubtedly very rare now. Its only one depleted copy is preserved at the National Library at Kolkata. Is it possible for it to be used by all for all the time? Realising the intensity of the problem, a microfilm copy of the newspaper has been made for use by many readers and researchers who can read it with the aid of microfilm-reader. The original copy is kept with care separately. The universal democratic right to use all the books and documents is thus safeguarded for the people of the new age.

In continuation of this line of thinking, a campaign has now started in America to ensure 'preservation and access'. With this objective, they have constituted at national level a 'Commission on Preservation and Access'. The term is very meaningful. It is indeed a new thought. Not only 'preservation', but opportunity to use it freely ('access') must be ensured. In many other countries of the world, this faith and idea are also gaining respect and recognition. With the aid of technological expertise, work in this new line has also started in India.

The headquarters of the 'Commission on Preservation and Access' in America has been set up in Washington in 1986. The objective of this Commission is to develop cooperation between different libraries and archives so that right preservation and easy availability for research of all types of printed and otherwise preserved documents can be arranged. The Commission also takes a leading role in developing joint project for preservation of books and documents through international cooperation. Maintaining the intellectual and cultural heritage is a sacred duty of the librarians and to help them in this respect with 'digital' technology the Commission has come forward with many projects. Keeping it in mind that 'excess acid' is causing maximum damage to books and documents and that for that reason millions of books and documents need mass deacidification and mass microfilming, the Commission has come forward to undertake preliminary survey in this matter in different countries. In countries like China, Germany, Ireland, Spain, Greece, France, Britain, Sweden, Netherlands, Canada and others, they have made survey of the quantum of damage caused to books and documents and the preservation methods taken by them to prevent such damages. Based on those surveys they have made the reports which are considered to be most valuable in the field of book preservation throughout the world.

Among the mass deacidification systems that have been introduced in different developed countries of the world, the most notable system among them is the 'polymerisation using low density gamma rays', which while removing the acidity of the papers, also helps regaining the strength of the papers. Besides this, the other method, adopted at the Library of Congress, known as DEZ, i.e., 'diethyl zinc process' is considered as very potential. But the main drawback about these processes is that these cannot be used in small scale. For installing the 'plant' for these processes we need to start work with at least 3 to 5 lakh books and documents. Naturally, financially or technologically most of the countries cannot afford to install such plants.

Besides 'mass deacidification', the other process that attracts us most is 'mass reformatting', among which the most popular and effective method is 'microfilming'. In case of old newspapers, 'microfisch' is also very popular in some places. Going one step forward from reformatting with microfilm, recent advancement is reformatting with CD-disk. Its advantage is this that from CD the documents can be directly transferred to computer memory, as a result of which we can instantly obtain together all the pages that we want.

But till now microfilm is largely used in most of the countries. Incidentally it may be mentioned that during the last nineties one Indo-American joint project of microfilming of Indian publications had started. The Library of Congress, USA submitted to the Government of India a concrete book preservation proposal relating to South Asia, including India. Accordingly, the Government of India gave its consent to the microfilming project for book preservation in May 1990. Thus started the MIPP, i.e., Microfilming of Indian Publications Project.

For this project, the National Bibliography of Indian Literature, edited by B.S. Kesavan and published by the Sahitya

Academy, has been accepted as the primary tool to identify the books for preservation. This Bibliography, in five volumes, has enlisted more than 60,000 titles published between 50 years from 1903 to 1953.

This MIP project also intends: (i) to compile a 'Machine readable bibliographic data base' for inclusion of all titles of the National Bibliography of Indian Literature (NBIL); and (ii) to microfilm all the books selected out of the NBIL. In general, all of the nineteenth and twentieth century publications of Indian literature are taken into account for this Project. It works in four major centres at Kolkata, Delhi, Chennai and Mumbai. Microfilming of documents in specified languages are being done in these centres. Indexing is also being done simultaneously. The project takes into consideration about 60,000 titles in 22 languages in India.

The working policy decision as taken by this joint Indo-American project is as such: (1) One Camera Master Negative and one Service Negative copy will be kept in one selected centre in India. (2) In the library of this centre in India will also be kept the documents' positive copy, along with the service copy for the users. (3) The MARC copy of the NBIL will be kept in each of the participating library so that its users can find out their desired documents. (4) At the same time, one Negative and one service copy will also be kept in the Library of Congress, USA. All these documents will be available everywhere in the world through Internet and other media.

It is reported that till 1994, 13 libraries took part in the project. Master Negative and Service Negative copies along with the positive copies are kept in the Central Secretariat Library in New Delhi.

Besides this joint MIP project, quite a few libraries in India are also working with their own preservation projects through microfilming. In National Library, Calcutta a few high quality foreign cameras are being used for this purpose on regular basis. This helps us to reach the new horizon of book preservation. We intend to move further through digitisation.

Incidentally, we may mention about some problems that have recently cropped up at the Esplanade unit (at the centre of the city) of the National Library, Kolkata, particularly in respect of microfilming of the old and rare newspapers stocked there. In fact, microfilming work could not be initiated there for various reasons, and as such the rich collection of nineteenth and twentieth century newspapers and periodicals located there has reached a very dangerous stage causing a serious threat to preservation of this written heritage of our country.

Before dealing further in the matter I may refer to a similar situation experienced in China. In 1991 (September 19 – October 12, 1991) a team of preservation specialists of US visited China to study the state of affairs of different public libraries and the book collections there. At the end of the visit the report that they have submitted ('Report of a visit to the People's Republic of China, by Hans Rütimann, March 1997') is most interesting and worth mentioning. The report states about a library there—'thousands of books and periodicals crumbling at a touch'. In another part of the Report it is stated—'A tour through the stacks (of Chongging Municipal Library), the reading room, and the rare book collection was depressing. Thousands of newspapers on shelf after shelf are in such advanced stages of deterioration that they look as if they had been pulled out of a fire. And these materials are still freely handed out to users. We watched readers turn the pages and break them, then either wipe the pieces off the table or put them in back between the pages'. During the recent past, a visit to the newspapers unit (at Esplanade, Calcutta) of the National Library, Calcutta revealed the same pathetic condition of its collections. The researchers there also have had the same experience as stated above. While turning the faded brittle pages of the old newspapers, they were breaking down and spreading over the table in small pieces, leaving no other way but to wipe them off or to put them back in between the pages. In such a situation we could only lament that these old brittle newspaper pages would no more be available as silent witness of the past. What a great loss to the nation!

To get rid of such odd situation the National Library authority has recently (November 2013) started taking strong measures to save our printed heritage. The entire old and rare newspaper collection, many portions of which have already started showing distinct signs of irreversible stain of acidification and degeneration, is now shifted to the well-equipped and dust-free clean air-conditioned environment of the Microphotography Division of Bhasha Bhavan located at the main Alipur campus of the National Library where all the content of the Old Newspaper Collection will be microfilmed, as well as digitised, helping its proper preservation for posterity. It is reported that the National Library has now acquired a state of the art 'Hybrid Microfilm Camera' which is capable of delivering both microfilms and digital images at the same go. So, we are hopeful about the prospect of best preservation.

These 8,000 odd bound volumes of newspapers are now not only assured of best preservation, but at the same time they will be available to the users in microfilmed and digitised format.

The National Library authority is reported to have stated that they have plans to convert the present space at the Esplanade Reading Room into a City Hub where the state of the art library services will be available to readers in microform and digital format. Apart from the old and rare newspapers and periodicals, more than 20,000 books which have already been digitised at the National Library are also expected to be made accessible at the City Hub.

Incidentally, it may be clarified that digitisation is the process of converting information into a digital format from other formats. Digitising information makes it easier to preserve, access and share, as explained by the experts. For example, they say, an original historical document may only be accessible to people who visit its physical location, but if the document content is digitised, it can be made available to people worldwide. There is a growing trend towards digitisation of historically and culturally significant data.

Thus, with the introduction and growing trend of microfilming and digitisation, we are moving towards the new horizon of book preservation.

13

LIS Education for Public Library Services in the Twentyfirst Century

Change in Concept of Public Library Services

Public libraries are sure to take a new shape and character in the Twentyfirst century. The process of change has already started. Even during the past few decades, there has been a sea change in the concept of public library services. This change has come not only in conceptual level, but also in technology for rendering library services. The traditional idea of library as a store-house of knowledge confined only within the pages of printed books is rather obsolete now-a-days, and obviously the librarian is also no more regarded as a mere keeper or custodian of books. Bidding farewell to the traditional custodian mentality, the librarian has to assume now-a-days the role of a social leader of the people around his neighbouring locality with the key task of satisfying their needs and demands for information—may be for educational, cultural or recreational purposes. To achieve this social task, the librarian has to collect, along with books, various other non-book materials (NBM) and audio-visual materials (AVM) which have proved to be essential tools for achieving his goal. Aided with these NBM and AVM tools the librarian can satisfy various information needs of his invitee clientele, many of whom are even illiterate.

Libraries turned to Library Resource Centres

NBM or AVM has now become important part of library collection. Particularly due to the fact that bulk of our population are still illiterate whom we aspire to serve and their needs and demands for information in their day-to-day life can best be satisfied through the media of NBM or AVM, like charts, maps, coloured posters and illustrations, micro-film, film, slides, cassettes, tapes, videos, gramophones, etc. Traditional public libraries are, therefore, now better termed as Library Resource Centres (LRC), having a collection of such multimedia resources to satisfy the varied needs of their users.

Extension Work of LRC assumes Wider Connotation

With the change and development of educational technologies, library science is also keeping pace with the changing scenario and adopting their newer tools, aids and techniques for its survival and development. In the coming days, in public libraries, particularly in rural public libraries in India, NBM and AVM will have an increasing role to play to serve the millions of our illiterate and neo-literate population, who are obviously having lesser capability to utilise printed books, but having a keen sense of understanding and appreciation of new ideas and techniques. We should better term them as 'unlettered', not 'illiterate'. Since public libraries are funded by contributions of all tax payers, how can they deny their services to the majority of the tax payers who are mostly unlettered.

In fact, by strengthening and extending the areas of public library services, we can strengthen the foundation of democracy in our country.

At one time in Europe even, public libraries, rather LRCs were used to be called 'Poorman's University'. The idea appears to be more relevant in our country where millions of people are still unlettered and lying below the poverty line. Rejuvenated modern public libraries, in true sense, can offer them all scope for self-development in respect of access to information, culture and recreation.

Extension Work converted to Outreach Programmes at LRC

Previously, we have had the practice of organising library extension work, as was conceived earlier, periodically or occasionally, i.e., at certain intervals in addition to normal book services, but LRC services are designed to offer book and non-book services, simultaneously as a daily routine work throughout the year NB and AV services of LRCs are no more considered as extension work they are now becoming vital part of regular library services closed integrating the book and non-book services. They can very well 'reach out' to the people incapable to step in the library premises, being physically ill or handicapped or confined within the prison cells. Such services are, therefore, very correctly termed outreach programmes which can contribute enormously for the upliftment of the society as a whole.

LRC Offers Most Socially Sensitive CIS

The non-book services offered by the public libraries of the LRCs include, besides outreach programmes and audio-visual services, another very important service, viz., information service. In the present day context, information service has wider connotation and far-reaching social impact. It is generally expressed as Information Referral Service (IRS) or popularly called as Community Information Service (CIS). An expert opinion explained it as 'a logical response to demonstrated need for non-book information about community resources'. (Clara S. Jones (ed.), *Public Library Information and Referral Service*, Gaylord Professional Service, 1978.)

Library Association of the UK have explained CIS as 'positive decision to concentrate on enabling people, particularly those in lower socio-economic groups, to act either individually or collectively on their problems in the fields of housing, employment, family and personal matters, consumer affairs, household finance, education, welfare rights and civil rights'. For further clarification, Library Association has defined CIS as 'service which assist individuals and groups with daily problem-solving and with participation in the democratic process. The services concentrate on the needs of those who do not have ready access to other sources of assistance and on the most important problems that people have to face, problems to do with their homes, their jobs and their rights'. [*Community Information—What Libraries can do: A Consultative Document*, London: Library Association, 1980.]

International Recommendation and Approval for NBM/AVM and CIS

Many of the international bodies, including the UNESCO or the IFLA (International Federation of Library Associations and Institutions) have recommended development of all such multi-faceted non-book services, along with the traditional book services, in public libraries for satisfying the growing needs of the society. In fact, it will not be too much of optimism to hope that this emerging new concept of public library will be a reality throughout the world by the beginning of the twentyfirst century. In such a situation LIS education must also adapt itself to the changing scenario to discharge its duties properly.

Before going into details of necessary changes that should be incorporated in LIS education system to suit the needs of the public libraries in the coming days, we may examine the relevant recommendations of the international bodies like UNESCO or IFLA in this respect. The most comprehensive definition of public library that has so far been given by the UNESCO, in cooperation with IFLA, in its Public Library Manifesto of 1994 is worth recollecting. It reads as follows: 'The Public Library, the local gateway to knowledge, provides a basic condition for lifelong learning, independent decision-making and cultural development of the individual and social groups. This manifesto proclaims

UNESCO's belief in the public library as a living force for education, culture and information'.

If we trace back a few earlier records, a more elaborate and clear idea may be obtained about the prospect of expanding public library services. 'The UNESCO Public Library Manifesto 1972' may be referred to in this context as a most valuable relevant document which recommends collection of NBM or AVM, along with books, in public libraries for developing education, culture and information services. Its relevant points are quoted below:

> 'Since the printed word has been for centuries the accepted medium for the communication of knowledge, ideas and information, books, periodicals, newspapers, remain the most important resources of public libraries.
> 'But science has created new forms of record and these will become an interesting part of the public library's stock, including print in reduced form for compact storage and transport, films, slides gramophone records, audio and video tape, for adults and children, with the necessary equipment for individual use and for cultural activities.'

IFLA guidelines for Public Libraries also recommend use of AVM in library services. It asserts: 'in no circumstances should audio-visual materials be regarded as an additional luxury in library provision; they are necessary components in a fully integrated library service, complementary to the printed word'. [IFLA Publications 362—*Guidelines for Public Libraries/prepared for the IFLA Section of public libraries*, Minchem, New York, 1986.]

IFLA further explains: 'In many instances audio-visual formats are more effective than their print based counterparts. For example, movement is more readily understood if it is portrayed by moving images on film or videotape, sound recordings are indispensable for the enjoyment of music; foreign languages are more easily learned through the medium of sound recordings'. [IFLA Publication 36.]

Another UNESCO publication asserts that AV materials instruct, enrich and entertain 'more dramatically and sometimes more effectively than printed materials'. [Campbell, H.C. *Developing Public Library Systems and Services.* Paris: UNESCO, 1983.]

Indian National Policy also Recommends use of NBM/AVM and CIS

The Committee on National Policy on Library and Information System under the chairmanship of Prof. D.P. Chattopadhyay submitted a report in May 1986, emphasising on the need to use AVM and introduce CIs in rural areas. The relevant portion of the report may be reproduced here:

> 'The most important task before the Government is to establish, maintain and strengthen the free public libraries in the country and enable them to work as a system.
>
> 'The main thrust in this area should go to the rural public library. A village or a village cluster with an adequate population should have a community library which will also serve as an information centre. Resources of different agencies engaged in the work of public health, adult education, local self-government and such others may be pooled to build up this composite centre...
>
> 'The community library should also importantly cater for adult education and make adequate audio visual aids available to attract the illiterate villagers.'

UNESCO Public Library Manifesto, 1994

But experimentation with multi-faceted role of public libraries never ends at any point of time. In view of fast progress of information technology and at the same time, enormous problems associated with growing needs of the common people for knowledge and information, library planners throughout the world go on changing, modifying or expanding their views on never ending scope of public library services. One very glaring example of such progress in thought has been explicitly reflected in the latest revision of the UNESCO manifesto, incorporating therein their latest thinking on the subject. We may refer here some of the relevant portions of this document, viz., UNESCO Public Library Manifesto 1994, which has been prepared in cooperation with the IFLA:

The Manifesto asserts—'collections and services have to include all types of appropriate media and modern technologies as well as traditional materials. High quality and relevance to local needs and conditions are fundamental'.

Among the various key emissions of the Public Library that the Manifesto has enumerated, the following are quite very relevant for our present study:

- 'ensuring access for citizens to all sorts of community information;
- 'providing adequate information services to local enterprises, associations and interest groups;
- 'facilitating the development of information and computer literacy skills; and
- 'supporting and participating in literacy activities and programmes, for all age groups, and initiating such activities, if necessary.'

Besides these vital missions of the public library, the Manifesto further suggests to take measures to 'ensure nationwide library coordination and cooperation' by promoting national public library network. The Manifesto also asserts to always emphasise on the 'local community needs, and to ensure all library services 'physically accessible to all members of the community' and at the same time, to organise 'outreach services for those unable to visit the library'. The Manifesto also suggests to take care that the library services are 'adapted to the different needs of the community in rural and urban areas'. Last, but not the least, it suggests that 'outreach and user education programmes have to be provided to help users benefit from all the resources'.

A Word of Caution, Too

As has been rightly pointed out by the UNESCO Manifesto, too, we must not forget that all such NBM/AVM or IT products will only be complementary to, and not substitute of, the traditional book materials in the public libraries.

Information Revolution characterises the twentyfirst Century

However, on careful examination of the aforesaid Manifesto, it is quite very evident that the UNESCO has correctly identified the information revolution that is currently sweeping the world and has judiciously assessed the impact that it is likely to make on every sphere of life with the beginning of the twentyfirst century. Obviously, public libraries will be no exception and in the forthcoming century they will also be equally influenced by the global information revolution. In view of such possible impact of information revolution, UNESCO has rightly made radical changes in its 1994 manifesto to adapt the public library services to the changing circumstances where it will be essential to facilitate the development of information and computer literacy skills in public libraries.

In fact, the change has already started coming in. Many of the advanced public libraries now provide internet access, CD-ROMS, wide area network and resource sharing facilities, personal computers (PC) or network computers (NC), multimedia with audio-visual facilities, dialogue information services and so on. The publisher of the magazine SPAN, in its recent issue (February-March 1997) has commented, the Internet and the World Wide Web (www) are a little like the great library in Alexandria, which in the fourth century contained all the world's information in one place. Only this time anyone anywhere will have access to it by computer. It will bring us all closer together.

Of late, public libraries in India, too, have just started getting in touch with the global information revolution. And we can reasonably expect, many of the Indian libraries will be equipped with state-of-the-art information technology by the beginning of the twentyfirst century.

LIS Education must also Adapt to the Changing Scenario

If that be the changing scenario of public library services in the forthcoming century, who are those professionals to man the future public libraries in India? Obviously, the responsibility lies with the Indian library professionals who are supposed to be the products of Indian Schools of Library and Information Service. In such a demanding situation our Library and Information Science (LIS) education system and its curriculum must be redesigned to keep pace with the information revolution and the consequent changing situation in the public library services. Many of the points suggested in the UNESCO Manifesto and other international and national policy documents and as discussed so far in our present study will no doubt prove to be quite relevant while redesigning our LIS syllabus. If the emergent new concept of public library and consequent new set of services based on new types of aids, tools, materials and technologies responding to the crying needs and demands of a new social order, are not adequately reflected in the LIS syllabus, we cannot expect to get the desired quality output of trained professionals from the LIS schools for organising our planned public library services in the forthcoming century. Hence, for implementing the desired objectives of building a network of modern public library services throughout the country our leaders and planners of LIS education, should immediately initiate revision of syllabus from the certificate to the post-graduate level so that we may be fully prepared to satisfy the twentyfirst century aspirations.

Basic Approach to the Revision of LIS Curriculum

While initiating revision of LIS syllabus, our basic approach should be to develop a modern LIS education system that can impart:

(i) Knowledge and acquaintance of various types, technology

and applications of NBM and AVM in public library services;

(ii) Primary knowledge, skill and appreciation of information technology and computers, in view of their multi-faceted applications in public library services;

(iii) Acquaintance with the techniques of outreach programmes; and

(iv) User education for proper utilisation of the available resources by the users' themselves.

In post-graduate level, there may be optional special papers for specialisation in public library services or others. Being a professional course, the syllabus must also be practice-oriented.

Above all, we must ensure that the students and trainees may develop an appreciation of, and mental aptitude for, this emerging new concept of public library services through our revised LIS education in the coming years.

LIS Education should Match our Social Needs

The new LIS education that we are aiming at for public library services in the twentyfirst century should develop in the wider perspective of the Library and the Society. We are now living in a society that urgently needs countrywide literacy drive and at the same time taking care for the neo-literates by carefully designing post-literacy programmes and feeding the neo-literates with suitable literature. Our society also needs a network of community information services to feed the urgent information needs of the millions of poor people in their day-to-day life and thus facilitating upgradation of their social status. All possible application of information technology and computers for the maximum benefit of public library users is also an urgent social need. Our public libraries of the twentyfirst century can play a vital role in satisfying all such social needs. We must, therefore, redesign our Library and Information Science education to suit all such social needs of the public libraries in the coming century.

We wonder, if, IT comes and develops so fast, can LIS education be far behind.

14

B.S. Kesavan and Five Laws of Librarianship

Padmashree B.S. Kesavan—the legendary figure in the library field of India—passed away on 16th February, 2000. While recollecting the various colourful incidents of his eventful life, the first thing that strikes me is the Five Laws of Librarianship that we can derive from his distinctive life-long library services. It is not that Kesavan himself had formulated any such laws, verbally or in writing, still it strikes me as because his entire working life appears to be a living symbol of librarianship. If we carefully study the multiplicity and depth of his life and work, we may clearly realise what is meant by librarianship. Of course, the meaning or the definition of librarianship that I have tried to formulate through 'Five Laws' is absolutely of my own thinking. Its essence or acceptability can be judged by library experts. Of course, I would like to admit at the very beginning that I have conceived of Five Laws of Librarianship in the backdrop or pattern of S.R. Ranganathan's Five Laws of Library Science. Ranganathan with golden touch of his vast intellect thoughts and merit had presented us in writing, his worldwide acknowledged theory and formulation of Five Laws of Library Science, which Kesavan through his life-long devotion to library services had taught us the concept of librarianship, which I have tried to formulate through Five Laws of Librarianship. In this matter, my role is like that of a garland-maker, as I have tried to knit together (like a garland) five 'letters', taking clue from Kesavan's achievements, to expose the concept of librarianship.

This garland of five 'letters', i.e., Five Laws can be expressed in a single English word— 'IDEAL'.

Where,
I – stands for Initiative,
D –stands for Drive,
E – stands for Expertise,
A – stands for Aptitude, and
L – stands for Learning, i.e., constant learning from experience.

Thus the word 'IDEAL' composed of Five Laws can give us an ideal definition of Librarianship. In other words, in order to be an ideal librarian or for rendering ideal library services, the aforesaid five qualities are essential. These qualities were profusely available in Kesavan, hence he was indeed an ideal librarian. He taught us through his life-long activities how to acquire these essential qualities or in other words, what is actually meant by Five Laws of Librarianship.

Library is a social institution. For achieving social welfare, its strength and potential are immense. Hence, it needs a lot of initiative and mental strength to build it up or to improve its standard of services. Precisely, I have tried to identify these necessary qualities and attainments as Five Laws. These qualities or laws are: Initiative, Drive, Expertise, Aptitude and Learning (i.e. a process of constant learning from experience). Once these qualities can be attained, then and only then one can transform a library into a strong multipurpose social institution or can raise the standard of its services up to an ideal level. In fine, we can designate virtues (in the field of library services) as Librarianship. B.S. Kesavan may not be the originator of these Five Laws, but he is the best exponent of these Five Laws. In India, he has developed a model of Librarianship—through his life-long library services.

Those who came in personal contact with Kesavan, they must be knowing how strong was his personality. A tall fair looking person like Bellari Samanna Kesavan could easily attract the people around him by virtue of his rare personality. Hardly we could find an eloquent speaker like him. He was born on 10th May, 1909 in a reputed Brahmin family of Mysore (presently Karnataka). He had his education in Mysore and London—mainly he studied English literature and thereafter Library Science in London University. He started his career as a Lecturer in English in Mysore University and then in a college at Bangalore. Then after doing for some time editorial work under CSIR, he joined the Education Department of the Government of India. His work-capabilities and personality actually started flourishing from 1948—when he took over as the first librarian of the National Library of free India in Calcutta. He was then 39 years old—along with his education and experience, and untiring zeal for creative work. With the wealth in his possession, he started reorganising the National Library. He shifted it to an entirely new environment. From the narrow space of 'Jabakusum House' on the Chittaranjan Avenue of Calcutta, the library jumped to the wide open space of Belvedere (which once housed the winter palace of the Governor General in Calcutta). Shifting of the National Library to such a place was at that time a most courageous work with outstanding foresight. Convincing the authority of the great importance of National Library in the cultural life of a newly freed developing country and thus occupying such a big prestigious space for the National Library was perhaps possible only for a personality like that of Kesavan. He could secure confidence of national leaders like Jawaharlal Nehru, Abul Kalam Azad, Humayun Kabir in this respect. It was the beginning of his characteristic 'Initiative' and 'Drive'. We can realise now how much necessary was this huge space like that of Belvedere for the purpose. National Library of an independent country should naturally be ever-growing. Hence, as we had such a big space like Belvedere, we could gradually construct many more buildings to accommodate many new needs of the growing library system—and its service network could also be expanded. An integrated overall planning, energetic initiative and high speed to implement those plans for building up a big size library—history proves that all these were evident in Kesavan's work for years together.

During the fifties and sixties of the last century—the post of librarian of the National Library (the post of Director was not created at that time) was the highest post in the field of library of the then India—Kesavan could make this convinced to the learned people of the society by means of his lively speed of work and administrative skills. Kesavan was the librarian there for fifteen years (1948-1963). Still now many people feel that it was the golden period of the National Library. The main reason being the lively presence of Kesavan. When he used to pass through the Reading Room, even the most attentive reader would have respectfully glanced at him for a moment. Whenever he used to visit different departments of the library (as was his regular habit), his colleagues used to become very alert. Through his keen eyes, he could easily detect any of the faults wherever that might be. The fault might be in respect of cataloguing or classification problem, or in respect of book acquisition or bibliography or in finding reason why a requisitioned book is not promptly reaching the reader, or in respect of cleanliness in the library building. In this respect 'expertise' was his main asset. With which was added his love for his colleagues, his sincerity in work and above all his strong personality. By virtue of these all, he could build up a consolidated team to render the appropriate library services. That team could maintain the high standard of services as well as the trend of development of the library for about two decades. It was Kesavan's credit that he could thus build up model standard of librarianship.

During his tenure at the National Library, Kesavan had another big contribution of initiating the Indian National Bibliography (INB), which started publishing from 1958. For determining the trend of Indian publications and for raising its quality to world standard this INB was essential. Kesavan had not only realised it, but at the same time, he made a planned programme for it and built up the necessary infrastructure to expedite its publication. There were many complicated problems for its execution. The variety of Indian languages, various types of alphabet and difficulty in its printing added to the problem and above all, there was bureaucratic resistance and problems of financial allocation. In spite of all such problems Kesavan succeeded in such an apparently impossible task, and at the root of his success was his 'initiative-drive-expertise', and obviously was added to it his typical 'attitude' as was necessary for improving the standard of library services. With an urge of such an 'aptitude' and by dint of strong personality Kesavan could rush to Delhi and convince the authorities about the necessity of INB and could get sanctioned for the purpose more than ten posts of 'gazetted rank' at one go. In the context of contemporary situation it was indeed an impossible task, but he could do it and had left for us the primary lesson of librarianship.

Librarianship is basically 'service'-oriented work. Joining this profession only for earning money and confining it only as a matter of profit and loss, 'aptitude' for librarianship can never be developed. Daily routine-work is there, but one ideal librarian must overcome it and set an example of model library services to satisfy the aspirations of the society. Kesavan had taught us this lesson throughout his library career.

While developing the National Library, Kesavan has set up an example of a model public library. Similarly, he had also shown us how to organise 'Special Library' or 'Science and Technology-based Library' services, while setting up an ideal national institute. He took up the charge as the first Director of the INSDOC (Indian National Scientific Documentation Centre) in Delhi in 1963. After working there for six years, he retired from government service in 1969. During these last six years in his government service, he once more presented a lesson to the librarians of new generation how to constantly learn from experiences ('constant learning process'). Thus his life-long devotion to work has presented us the essential lesson of librarianship. I have drawn from this lesson the 'Five Laws of Librarianship'.

Even after retiring officially, his source of strength, energy and capabilities was not exhausted. Hence Kesavan kept himself engaged in many new activities for next few years. He once again joined teaching in Delhi University. With invitation from abroad, he went to Bangkok and then to Teheran with UNDP assignment. During the last years, he was engaged in writing books, resulting in publication of his outstanding work *History of Printing and Publishing in India*, published by National Book Trust in five volumes. A great scholar-librarian like B.S. Kesavan most efficiently proved that research and writing can also be an integral part of librarianship.

B.S. Kesavan is still alive among his numerous admirers. He continues to inspire librarians of future generation. From his life-long achievements in the field of library services we could formulate the Five Laws of Librarianship—IDEAL.

15

Reading Habit – New Challenges

Future Perspectives and Development of Book Culture

In the present day context, growth or decline of reading habits is more a social phenomenon than individual pursuit. And the society we are living in is fast changing. More characteristically, present day society or the world is fragmented and the human life, too, is fragmented. From such 'fragmented world and fragmented lives comes the biggest challenge to the book and book reading', says Zygmunt Bauman, the renowned Emeritus Professor of Sociology, University of Leeds (UK). Prof. Bauman further concludes: 'The fate of the book in our globalising world does not depend on, and cannot be explained by, technologies of printing or anything else confined to the publishing trade. Books share the fate of the societies of which they are a part. When we worry about the future of books and book readership, let us take a closer look at society and its trends. To make books fit for the society we inhabit, let us try to prevent it from becoming unfit for books.' [Contribution to '100-day dialogue' on "What has happened to Reading", conducted online by 'The Book and the Computer' in the year 2000.]

This is true, because Society and Books are quite very linked with each other. Barring a few glorious exceptions, books are as much creative products of individuals, as of the society surrounding them. They influence each other to achieve the goal of creativity. Books are, therefore, generally considered as mirror of the society, while at the same time, quite a few immortal books have played the revolutionary role of changing the society, classic examples of which being *Uncle Tom's Cabin*, *Mother*, *Good Earth*, *Das Kapital* or *Nildarpan*, *Anandamath* and others in Bengali. With the same analogy, reading of books may also be treated as a social phenomenon, which is obviously, therefore, supposed to be changed with the change of social trends. In the present day society where traditional moral values have changed drastically, why not a change of reading habits should be expected too. And, in fact, it has changed. But how far, and where it is leading to in future—we are all pondering that.

While pondering the nature of such change in reading habits, let us first clarify further the basic characteristics of reading habits. As we have already pointed out, social factor is one of the major factors affecting the reading habits. But there are other factors, too. Basically, reading habit is a mental faculty which is developed and indeed influenced by the individual's family and social environment, his literacy standard, his needs and aspirations, and availability of resources, and, of course, by his inner urge and liking and at the same time, the distracting forces working around him. Hence, for analysing the future perspective, reading habit should be studied in its entirety.

In course of such study, we come across various types of reading, such as: (i) Life-long reading, (ii) Reading for pleasure, entertainment and peace, (iii) Reading for knowledge—being a learning process, (iv) Reading for information—including information for livelihood—to satisfy various information needs, (v) Casual reading—reading for temporary needs (*e.g.*, issue-based reading, like reading of election campaign literature and others), and (vi) Daily reading—newspapers, magazines, trade or business papers, etc.

But these types should never be treated as water-tight compartments. They are always overlapping, with extension of one to the other or conversion of one into another. But all that we are concerned in the present context, is the volume of reading materials that is produced now-a-days in different countries and in different languages—to satisfy such reading habits. More specifically, we are concerned whether this volume of reading materials is declining or growing, whether the number of readers is increasing or decreasing—irrespective of the availability of resources. Our other significant concern is also about the relative strength of the media—whether print media or the electronic media are comparatively gaining more strength and popularity than the other. Perhaps, here lies the origin of our thinking—whether printed books are still having a bright prospect or they are destined to face a gloomy future under the threat and challenge of the emergence of television, particularly the Internet.

It may not be an easy task to find out a universally acceptable clear-cut pointed answer to all these queries or issues, as the situation varies from country to country and even the survey based statistics available on these issues very often contradict each other. It is, therefore, difficult to have a clear whole view of a nation's reading habit. Vision of two ends of its image is obscured by contradictory statistics and biased views. 'The image that comes to mind is that of a giant who stands with his feet in the mud and his head thrust high into the clouds. The mud and clouds obscure one's view of him.'

There is a general feeling, if not a bias, amongst many of the intellectuals that with the emergence of e-media, particularly with the widespread of TV sets, from black & white to colour sets, people are spending lesser time for reading books and devoting more and more time to TV watching. But the available statistics on TV-viewing and reading of books do not support this contention. By and large, TV-viewing is not necessarily a compelling factor to adversely affect reading habits, as is evident from the situation in many countries, say, in UK—where at one recent point of time there were 16 different TV channels, yet the reading habit was not reported to have declined, rather has increased in the past two decades. Similarly in USA, Annual Index of American Public Library Circulation, as compiled yearly by the University of Illinois Library Research Centre, shows that the number of items checked out of public libraries has gone up consistently throughout the 1990s. Moreover, juvenile circulation has also increased.

Another recent American study has also revealed some interesting features of American life, viz., (i) TV viewing has little effect on academic achievements, (ii) Extreme TV watching takes place in low-income households, (iii) If your home life is one of severe deprivation, your reading and study habits will be affected. It is more a social problem than a cultural one.

In China today, the on-going liberalisation of Chinese society is having an equally liberating effect on books and reading. With fewer government restraints today, the number of books published in China is soaring and reading is more popular than ever.

But the situation in Japan is somewhat different. Here, as in America, books have become commodified by the consumer culture. Muro Kenji, Editor-in-Chief, 'The Book and the Computer' says, 'In Japan, where consumerist culture is in full stride, many have observed that sales of serious contemporary literature, literary classics, and scholarly works in the humanities and social sciences have fallen precipitously in recent years. In Europe and North America, one hears a similar claim: that the commercial and academic publishers who have traditionally specialised in books of this sort now face severe financial hardship. Driving this trend are several factors, including consolidation in the publishing industry, a focus on best sellers, and the allure of other media, such as television, radio, film and most recently, the Internet. Whatever the soundness of these claims, and whatever the causes of the trend they identify, one thing is beyond dispute: our reading habits are changing'. And, by and large, the majority of opinion is: decline in sales of serious books is indeed a worldwide development. But why should we lament over it particularly, as this happens to be the order of the day. Attendance to serious public lectures or seminars has also gone down appreciably. We should look forward to remedies elsewhere. We still have the ray of light, as there is no dearth of serious writers and there appears to have no problem for their contributions to be published regularly, although in smaller copies by 'print-on-demand' technology. Incidentally, this appears to be an interesting point that while one aspect of technology threatens the prospect of printed books, another aspect of technology comes for rescue of printed book culture.

The problem of declining reading habits in India is, however, not so alarming yet, as was generally apprehended in some circles. The National Policy on Education 1986 has rightly emphasised on book promotion, which says: 'Measures will be taken to improve the quality of books, promote the reading habit and encourage creative writing'. If the policy is followed with sincere efforts, the problem of declining reading habits can perhaps be averted. The available reports indicate that in 1950, only about 50 titles were produced, while the present figure has gone up to 67,000 titles per year. Moreover, Fiction forms about 10 per cent of the total annual publication and of late, demand for non-fiction books is increasing. About 16,000 publishers are also reported to operate in India presently.

The other aspect of the problem is also worth consideration. The majority of our people, about 70 per cent of our population, are rural based. And the tentacles of e-media have not yet reached the roots of our rural population. It may, therefore, be reasonably concluded that the e-media is yet to reach the majority of our population (only 0.5% of our total population are net-user). Moreover, the prevailing poverty in our country is still a contributing factor to slow down the march of e-media to all the remote corners of our rural life. Still 35.97 per cent (in 1994) of our people are living below the poverty line, and obviously, this bulk of our poorest population cannot afford to enjoy the facilities of e-media. They are still exposed to the traditional field of print media as before, and moreover, with the increasing trend of literacy in our country (65.38% in the year 2001), more and more people are gradually attaining capability to read (and write). In view of such rural-based situation of our country we need not be unnecessarily concerned about the decline in reading habits in near future.

But still, it must be admitted that India is no exception to the world trend of reading habit, which is having some localised phenomenon along with some universal development. After going through reports of different studies conducted in different countries, we have rather reasons to conclude that reading habit is neither declining, nor growing, but it is undergoing transformation — as to how we read and what we read.

In spite of divergent views, unanimity of opinion is found at least in respect of certain trends which may be summarised as such: (1) Reading habits have undergone a change. (2) Number of readers of 'serious' books is declining, while 'light' reading is the most favoured trend. (3) But 'serious' titles continue to be published as before, if not in bigger numbers, but smaller number of copies are printed. (4) Books have undergone 'transformation'—in physical formats, but continue to coexist, e.g., printed books and e-books—like CD-ROM, Internet, etc. The other aspect of 'transformation' in content and outlook may also attract our attention. As mentioned before, the life and the world is now fragmented—the fragmented world has wiped out continuity and long-term thinking. Books produced in such a situation tend to move from the universe of enlightenment to that of entertainment, change from durable values to the objects of consumption. We, therefore, witness giant book fairs on international and national levels, with the paradox of rising attendance to such book fairs coinciding with rapidly falling avid readership. Of course, there are exceptions with thoughtful production and readership, but this 'light' trend and erosion of values cannot be overlooked. The cult of 'best seller' lists—the 'hot books' read by 'everyone' and adorning 'everyone's' coffee table only to be thrown from the sitting room the next week when pushed out of fashion by the next best seller—signals the transformation of book into commercial commodity.

This is indeed a very disappointing feature of present day 'book culture'. But its originating cause cannot be attributed to 'screen culture', rather it is the product of current social trend. The various contributing factors that might have worked behind this trend include—consumerism, time-pressure and active lifestyle, erosion of moral values and others. For revitalising the book culture, we must, therefore, look deep into the social causes and make amends therefor.

But on the other hand, if it is argued that electronic media, like TV, is standing in the way of growth of reading habit—causing a decline in the worldwide publication trend, then we must assess whether any of the different types of reading as mentioned before (like reading for entertainment/enlightenment/knowledge/information/mental peace, etc.) or which of these types of reading are susceptible to be affected by the onslaught of e-media. A careful examination of the issue will reveal that, barring entertainment and news programmes at the backdrop of visual presentation on TV-screen, other types of reading continue to be equally relevant as before in the lives of the people and hence we need not be so sceptical or worried about the much-publicised likely decline in reading habits. Rather we are hopeful about a prosperous future for reading habits, which is reasonably expected to go up with the increasing population and their growing literacy, but all that we shall have to look after is to devise a method for converting this increasing trend of reading habit into a healthy book culture that will make humanity richer with peace and happiness.

While summing up various opinions of learned scholars across the countries, Muro Kenji, Editor-in-Chief, 'The Book and the Computer', says that presently books are becoming commodified, reading is being redefined as consumption, and the Internet is unleashing a deluge of text. These trends are linked to the decline of a shared public culture in many countries. In the backdrop of such disappointing trend, scholars now take a pragmatic view. They point out that movies, which could once be viewed only in theatres, can now be seen at home on video. They likened this to the situation with books, which once existed only on paper, printed hundreds or thousands of copies at a time. Now there is new pathway to the book-reading experience, one provided by the new technologies of online publishing, print-on-demand and the e-book. There will henceforth be two forms of the book, printed and electronic, the latter being built on the tradition of the former. This causes a transformation of reading habit in the current age.

In view of this apparent conflict between 'book culture' and 'screen culture', we wonder whether the electronic text will replace the many forms of the printed codex—book, magazine, newspaper, and so forth. The more likely reasonable possibility is the co-existence of the two in the decades to come. In a future that is already upon us, it is for us to determine, collectively, how best to utilise the new media.

There is no denial of the fact that in some areas the new media are better, more easily accepted by younger people, and even cheaper. A CD-ROM containing a whole dictionary with easy-to-click references or the entire contents of four of Europe's major art museums is indeed an attractive alternative to a bulky and costly set of print volumes. Researchers can also get tremendous help and benefit through Internet. Sitting quietly at home, they can search and obtain hundreds of printout of their subject—information from the whole world. Why should we then discard it?

On the other hand, printed book offers some unique privilege not available elsewhere. It is portable, browsable and can be used alone in any cosy comfortable corner of home or outside. Anybody, irrespective of age or wealth, can derive immense pleasure and peace from the book. It can be his life-long partner, even when he is deserted by all. How can we ignore it?

Perhaps, the best answer for the future, is the co-existence of the two. That is the way we can face the new challenge and sustain and develop the book culture in the years to come, Reading habits will thus continue to keep men more knowledgeable, more enlightened, better informed and better entertained. Crises of shrinking reading habits, if any, can surely be overcome in the domain of an enriched book culture. Earlier prediction of death of cinema with the advent of TV has not been proved true. For hundreds of years, people have bemoaned the end of 'serious' culture—yet culture survives. People have surmounted past cultural crises by redirecting the forces of crisis. Worldwide scholars associated with the aforesaid '100-day dialogue' are of the opinion that we can now do the same with the forces that have separated people from the act of reading in recent years—we can redirect them towards a renewal of the power of reading.

Before we conclude, we may mention about a specialised form of printed books which have been attracting more and more readers and thereby helping to develop the book culture as a whole. Obviously, we mean the paperback editions which have been, of late, very popular throughout the world. While explaining the phenomenon, a Paris-based senior journalist explained that a 1990 study showed, on the one hand, a drop in the number of "avid" readers (those who read more than 25 books a year) from 22 per cent in 1973 to 17 per cent in 1988, and on the other hand, an increase among "casual" readers (who read less than 10 books per year) from 24 per cent to 32 per cent. These casual readers read more because they read less expensively, with the market for paperbacks hardly being hurt. Of the 413 million books sold in 1996 (in France), 33.9 per cent (i.e. one-third) were paperbacks *versus* 31.7 per cent in 1988. This increase may be due to the fact that readers often wait for a paperback to come out, as they do for the television screening of some films.

General readers, of course, prefer this paperback and pocketbook edition not only for lower cost, but also for easy handling and for availing reading facilities in a present day faster life or in some odd situations, with the motto—'read while travel' in fast-moving cars, trains and airplanes. These thin handy editions cannot be categorised as degradation of book culture, rather it is an adjustment to suit the needs of the day and thereby achieving a new dimension in our traditional book culture. But, of course, I am afraid we do not venture to go for 'read and throw-away culture', just like hundreds of throw-away packages and one-time-use utility goods. Let us hope, more and more innovative book productions will be developed to face the challenge of the day.

16

Whether Reading Habit is under Adverse Pressure?*

About five hundred and fifty years have passed since the introduction of printed books. But the habit of writing, printing and reading books still now continues unabated. Very often various adverse conditions have developed. At the pressure of war-epidemic-flood-earthquake-partition-riot-famine, etc., books have very often appeared to be merely a negligible element. But overcoming all sorts of odd effects, a continuous flow of books had all along been maintained. As the taste of books is like that of divine water. Once you have tasted it, you cannot forget it, you cannot forego it. Books have moved along with civilisation, civilisation have developed along with books. Books have made our life meaningful. Particularly, when a man is alone, only reading-habit can give him the relief. Who can resist this eternal flow of relief and life.

But of late, there are apprehensions, whether reading-habit is now declining and whether the world of books and culture is decaying? As because the fight today is against technology. There has been unprecedented development in the field of printing and publication through various wonderful technology, but at the

---

* This issue has been referred to in the 100 days' worldwide online discussion on 'reading habits' conducted on behalf of "Books & Computers" in the year 2000.

same time this technology has created many alternatives to books, viz., computerised books, CD-ROM, Website, Internet and others. Now the question, how far the traditional books and reading habits are affected by all such technological attraction. It cannot be denied that the reading-habit is now facing a big challenge. Still the question remains, whether reading-habit is declining or rather changing?

In the present age, the increase or decline of reading-habit is more due to social factors than merely a personal matter. The society of the present day is changing fast or in other words, our society or the world or the life as a whole appears to be broken down in pieces and floating around, nowhere these are closeted together and stand in still. In the midst of this restless situation, the books or the habit of reading books are facing a big challenge. These remarks are made by Zygmunt Bauman, the renowned Professor of Social Science in the Leeds University of Britain. With these remarks Prof. Bauman concludes that in the percentage the fate of books is no more depending on printing technology or publishing art, that is now linked with social trends or its characteristics. Hence, while assessing the position of books or the habit of reading books, we must think of the present trend of the society. If we wish to make the books suitable for the society, where we are living, should rather try to see that our society does not become unsuitable for books.

In fact, books and society are closely interlinked. Although there are a few bright exceptions, but in general books are as much creation of personal talent, so much also creation of the surrounding society. The trend of this creation is continuing with mutual influence. Hence, books are very often called the mirror of the society. On the other hand, there are a few outstanding books which have caused revolutionary changes in the society, e.g., *Uncle Tom's Cabin*, *Mother*, *Good Earth*, *Das Kapital* or in Bengali literature *Neel Darpan*, *Anandamath*, *Pather Davi*, etc. In a similar way, it may be said that just like books, habit of reading books is also dependent on social system. With the change in society, reading habit also changes. Hence, as we now notice so many changes in traditional values in society, then the changes in reading habits is also quite natural. But the question remains, how far this change has taken place, or how far that change will lead us in future. With deep introspection, we can realise that besides social influence, some other influences also work on reading-habits. As for example, we may cite the influencing factors like family environment of the person, his standard of education, his personal needs and aspirations, availability of tools, surrounding obstacles, and above all his mental urge. Reading-habit develops on the combination of all these factors. There are various types of this habit, viz. (1) life-long reading, (2) reading for deriving mental peace and pleasure, (3) reading for acquiring knowledge, (4) reading for obtaining information necessary for livelihood, (5) reading for casual interest like that of election manifesto, pulse polio literature, etc., (6) daily reading materials like newspapers, share market quotations and other market news, literary supplements, etc. Now the question remains, whether the number of all such reading materials published in different languages is increasing or declining and at the same time whether the number of their readers is also increasing or declining. Besides these, we need to further analyse which one among the print and electronic media is leading in respect of number or popularity and in the perspective we are concerned to know the future of the printed books and others which are facing a big challenge of the Television-Internet world.

It is not very easy to get clear answers to these questions. The answer that we may get will differ from country to country. Even the contradictory answers and figures that we may get in this respect can obviously confuse us. A tendency of being biased in the matter can also not be denied. In fact, that very complicated issue is like a very big giant, whose feet are pressed deep inside the soil and his head is covered in the midst of high altitude clouds. The soil and the cloud together have made his full identity indistinct.

It is a common belief that due to the influence of widespread electronic media, particularly the black and white and coloured

TVs, people are now sparing lesser time in reading books, whereas more time is spent for enjoying TVs. But this idea or belief is not supported by facts and figures obtained from different countries. We may take the examples of technologically advanced countries say, England—where simultaneously more than 16 TV channels were in operation long before, still the reading-habit of the people had not declined there, rather that had increased during the last two decades. Similarly, we may consider the case of America. There the 'Library Research Centre' of Illinois University has edited and published one "Annual Index of American Public Library Circulation", which shows that the number of lending books from America's Public Libraries has systematically increased during the last nineties. Besides that, the lending of children's books has also increased.

A few recent survey reports of America have revealed some interesting facts. As for example, (1) Studies in schools have not been adversely affected due to introduction of TVs. (2) TVs are used more among the low-income families. (3) The more deprivation and lack of peace occur within the families, the more reading-habits are disturbed. Hence, it is evident that the problem of reading-habit is more a social than a cultural one.

In recent times, it is also observed in China that the more 'free thinking' is prevalent, the more liberal is the rate of publishing, as well as the reading-habit. State-control is now less there, resulting in increase in number of book-publishing and people's interest in reading books has also increased.

But the situation in Japan is somewhat different. Like in America, in Japan too, consumerism culture has widely spread and hence books are treated here as commodities. As per the opinion of Mr. Muro Kenji, Chief Editor of the aforesaid seminar on 'Books and Computers', "in recent times consumerism culture in Japan has reached the peak, as a result of which sale of serious modern literature, old classical literature or research publications on humanism and social sciences has gone down. On similar reasons, publishers of commerce and text books are facing serious financial crisis in Europe and North America. Trend of publication of 'best sellers' has increased, as well as attractions for TV-Radio-Cinema-Internet have also increased. There may be difference of opinion in this respect, but one thing is certain that our reading habit is gradually changing". It is evident throughout the world that the number of publishers and readers of serious books is going down. We need not be surprised at it. Because it is the trend of the modern age. The audience of serious talks or seminars are also declining. Still we have reasons for complacency or hopes elsewhere. Still there is no dearth of serious or research-oriented writers and the scope for publishing them regularly is still there. The change that has taken place is that only a limited number of necessary copies are printed. For this, a new technique of printing has developed, which is called 'print-on-demand' technology. Interestingly, as this recent development of technology has created a crisis in book-printing but at the same time it has helped to maintain the culture of printed books uninterrupted.

However, in comparison to other countries, crisis is not so acute in India. In our 1986 Declaration of 'National Policy on Education', considerable emphasis was given on book production, stating therein that encouragement would be given for upgradation of standard of books, development of reading habits and creative writings. If this policy is sincerely implemented, the problem of decaying reading-habits can be solved to a great extent. This can be substantiated by a few data. In 1950, the total number of annual publication in India was only 50, which increased to 67,000 in 2005. Out of this, novels were about 10 per cent, and demand for other types of books has also increased by now. In 2005, India had about 16,000 publishers.

Besides this, there is another factor which has caused to reduce the adverse effect of technology on reading-habits. In our country, about 70 per cent of our population are from rural areas, where e-media are still now comparatively weak. Only 0.5 per cent of our population are using internet. [Of late, of course, there is some increase in this percentage.] Besides this, the influence of poverty can also not be denied. 35.97 per cent of our population (as per 1994 figures) are living below poverty line, who are obviously out of the influence of e-media. But as the literacy rate is gradually increasing (which was 65.38% as per 2001 Census), the influence of traditional print-media is still now stronger.

Still it must be admitted that India's trend is no exception from the worldwide trend of reading-habits. But the worldwide survey in this regard reveals that the reading-habit is neither growing, nor declining, it is rather changing—in what way we are reading or what we are reading, that is now changing.

In spite of varying opinions, we may agree on certain points about the present trend of reading-habits, viz. (1) there has been change in reading-habit, (2) the number of readers of serious books is decreasing, while that of light books is increasing, (3) in spite of it, the publication of serious books still now continues unabated, rather growing further, although lesser number of copies are now printed, (4) external features of books have now changed and there is co-existence of traditional printed books and the present day e-books, like CD-ROM, internet and others. Change in contents or standpoints is also noticeable. Trends of knowledge to recreation, traditional values to consumerism are continuing side by side. As a result, large size book-fares are being held at national, as well as international levels, and it is further noticed that increasing number of people are attending there, while the number of intensive readers is gradually declining. As an exception, there is no dearth of thoughtful books or serious readers, but at the same time huge presence of light books or remarkable lack of sense of values cannot be denied. List of largely-selling books is becoming longer. Attractive 'hot' books are decorating more and more tea-tables, but very shortly they are pushed out as old stock by the incoming new set of 'hot' books. In such a situation, books are just becoming commodities.

This type of present day 'book culture' is really very disappointed. But for its development 'screen culture' cannot be blamed. It has its origin in the current social conditions. Various social diseases like consumerism, pressure of time, busy life style, decaying sense of values, etc., are influencing it. To get rid of it, we shall have to look for the sources of such social diseases. We need to cleanse the society to regain the life of books.

It is already stated how many types of 'reading' are there. How far TV can interfere in it. In TV, recreational pictures and news items attract the audience mostly. Besides this, there is plenty of time to devote for books. Hence, we need not worry about attraction and time for books. Particularly, when literacy rate is going up and simultaneously the population is also growing, then the chances of increasing number of readers cannot be denied. Then the only requirement is to correlate this increasing number of readers with a healthy aptitude for reading and the book culture. Humanity will then be richer after having the taste of happiness and peace.

The essence of all such research is that reading-habit is being changed. Previously, we could see the films at the cinema hall, now we can see it in video/TV at our homes. Similarly, we had before books only in print media—when thousands of copies could be printed at a time. The situation has now changed with development of new technology. To satisfy our reading-habit we have now books 'online', 'print-on-demand' and 'e-book'. Electronic media have now joined hands with traditional print media. As a result of which 'reading-habit' has now changed to new format. For days to come, both will continue simultaneously.

Of course, many amongst us prefer electronic media. Because wherever it is available, it costs less and particularly the young generation have preference to it. One large-size dictionary, or a multi-volume encyclopaedia or even the entire matter of the industrial museums of four European metropolitan cities can now be kept confined within a tiny CD-ROM and can easily be used as per needs. Then we need not have to cross over the hillock of huge collection of costly printed books at home. Researchers are now in a position at home to obtain important information and articles from far away libraries abroad through internet printouts. Why should we not take advantage of this unique reading-habit?

On the other hand, of course, printed books are also having some distinct advantages which are not available elsewhere. It can be easily carried to any place of our choice, whenever necessary we can easily browse over it and above all, we can read it alone, at home or outside, with all the pleasure. Irrespective of age or wealth, anybody can derive pleasure and peace by reading books of his choice. Books can be our life long companion, if everybody deserts books can still save us from curse of loneliness. How can we ignore such a friendly book?

In fact, both these media will safeguard our future. Once we had apprehension that cinema will be ousted with the advent of TV. But that has been proved to be wrong. Similarly, both print and electronic media will continue to co-exist without interference. Thirst for reading will remain alive forever. Reading of books and book culture will thus continue to flourish. Facing challenges of all sorts of adverse factors, reading-habit will continue to impart more knowledge, more clarity of thoughts, more information, more source of pleasure and entertainment. Reading-habit has not declined, will not decline and the books will continue to survive forever. Very often people lament for decadent culture, still revival of culture in new forms has never stopped.

Before we conclude, we must mention about a new format of printed books which is having increasing demand, people are buying and reading more such books. Obviously, we are referring to 'paperback' editions or cheaper editions of printed books. This has become popular throughout the world.

These thinner and lighter editions should not be treated as derogation of books, rather be treated as a suitable substitution to satisfy some specific needs. It is a challenging new addition in the field of traditional printed books. But for heaven's sake, these should not be treated as 'read and throw' types, like the 'use and throw' types. To meet the challenge of changing times, the type or colour or format of books are undergoing creative changes. The continuing stream of reading-habit is constantly making our likes richer.

Index